# Twenty-four Carrot Faith

## Still More Sermons From a Potato Field

Edgar (Ted) Stubbersfield

ISBN: 0-6486781-0-5
ISBN-13: 978-0-6486781-0-6

# DEDICATION

To my mate Freddy Kornis and (dare I say) his long suffering wife Barbara. "Glory!"

1 Cor. 9:16. Woe is me if I preach not the gospel

# CONTENTS

| | | |
|---|---|---|
| | Acknowledgments | i |
| 1 | Introduction to Acts | Pg 1 |
| 2 | When Life Interrupts Our Plans | Pg 9 |
| 3 | Ruth Gleans in Boaz's field | Pg 17 |
| 4 | A Church that Knows the Gospel | Pg 27 |
| 5 | The Parable of the Tractor | Pg 38 |
| 6 | Lessons from the Early Church | Pg 41 |
| 7 | Two Types of Farmers | Pg 54 |
| 8 | Woe is Me | Pg 57 |
| 9 | Truly, Truly I say unto you | Pg 68 |
| 10 | Grace and Peace in Abundance | Pg 80 |
| 11 | Joseph | Pg 90 |
| 12 | Monergism | Pg 99 |
| 13 | Ecclesiastical Supply Company | Pg 111 |
| 14 | Isaiah and Christian Mission | Pg 112 |
| 15 | Rahab's Washing, Ironing and Mending | Pg 122 |
| 16 | I Know a Little Greek, He's a Great Tiler | Pg 126 |
| 17 | The Tabernacle of David | Pg 133 |
| 18 | Principals of Living By Faith | Pg 143 |
| 19 | The Jewish Question | Pg 152 |
| 20 | A Prayer for the Reader | Pg 163 |
| | About the Author | Pg 164 |

# ACKNOWLEDGMENTS

Thanks and appreciation are due to the faithful and longsuffering brothers and sisters at Tenthill Baptist Church and other places in the Lockyer Valley in Queensland, Australia who gladly heard the laymen whose sermons are included in this book..

# 1 INTRODUCTION TO ACTS

*Pastor Iain was planning to do a series from the Book of Acts and asked me to prepare an introduction to the book.*

*Reading*: Acts 1: 1-11

[1] In my former book, Theophilus, I wrote about all that Jesus began to do and to teach [2] until the day he was taken up to heaven, after giving instructions through the Holy Spirit to the apostles he had chosen. [3] After his suffering, he presented himself to them and gave many convincing proofs that he was alive. He appeared to them over a period of forty days and spoke about the kingdom of God. [4] On one occasion, while he was eating with them, he gave them this command: "Do not leave Jerusalem, but wait for the gift my Father promised, which you have heard me speak about. [5] For John baptized with water, but in a few days you will be baptized with the Holy Spirit."

[6] Then they gathered around him and asked him, "Lord, are you at this time going to restore the kingdom to Israel?"

[7] He said to them: "It is not for you to know the times or dates the Father has set by his own authority. [8] But you will receive power when the Holy Spirit comes on you; and you will be my witnesses in Jerusalem, and in all Judea and Samaria, and to the ends of the earth."

[9] After he said this, he was taken up before their very eyes, and a cloud hid him from their sight.

[10] They were looking intently up into the sky as he was going, when suddenly two men dressed in white stood beside them. [11] "Men of Galilee," they said, "why do you stand here looking into the sky? This same Jesus, who has been taken from you into heaven, will come back in the same way you have seen him go into heaven."

## Introduction

Over coming weeks Pastor Iain is going to bring a series of messages to us drawn from the Book of Acts. I believe he is going to look primarily at what the Lord wants his disciples to do. The task set before me today is to give an introduction to the Luke's account of the early church.

I have in my hand a Gideon New Testament, small and if I put it in my pocket it is no more obtrusive than a packet of cigarettes. Both now are socially unacceptable, probably the Testament more so. But cast your mind back to first century Rome where things were a little different. Books did not exist and they wrote on papyrus scrolls, and the standard scroll was 10 metres long and about 300 mm wide. This was about as much as a single person could handle comfortably. Luke's gospel and his history of the early church are each crafted to fill an entire scroll. Josephus in his book one of *Against Apion* concludes it by saying, "I have run out of space and will have to start a second scroll." Unlike him, Luke did not start on row one, line one and say, "I wonder where this is heading", as often happens with my books. He had a target, the last line of the last row, 10 metres away and he was careful with what he included and excluded. So, what was Luke trying to say? Plenty, but I am only going to touch on three areas.

Luke writes with the keen observation that you would expect from a skilled medical professional. But it is not a history book as we know it. Rather than record history, Luke interpreted it and, in interpreting history, the Book of Acts represents the theology of the new church. He writes as an evangelist proclaiming the gospel of Jesus, in his first work interpreting his earthly career and, in the second, his exalted career and of his kingdom's invasion of this world's uttermost parts. So as not to overshoot his target, Luke left things out such as Paul's missionary trip to Illyricum (Rom 15:19). So, with his obvious care about the length of the work, we should see his repetitions as pointing us to pivotal events in the Church's history. These repetitions are Paul's conversion (mentioned three times) and Peter with Cornelius. Both those events, Paul's calling to be the apostle to the Gentiles and the Spirit falling on Gentiles under Peter, are part Luke's recording of the transition from "The Way" as our faith was first called by the Jewish believers when it was seen as a sub group under Judaism to the separate Gentile Christian church. It was a painful transition at times.

**Point 1 A gospel with the power to save sinners**

Early on, as the church was growing in Jerusalem many priests and teachers of the Law were converted. What was the response when gentiles were starting to get converted? They had to be brought under the umbrella of Judaism and observe the Law just like them. The religious Jewish elite looked down on their own people and could say, "this mob that knows nothing of the law—there is a curse on them" (John 7:49). The reaction of most Palestinian Jews to Gentiles who were living in a bubble was one of contempt and separation. But there were people attracted to the Jewish faith because of its ethical God and ethical living and the reaction to them was varied. Some were accepted, probably most were wary and one comment we find in the Babylonian Talmud was that "converts are as injurious to Israel as an open sore" (Babylonian Talmud, Yevamot 47b).

But in Acts we see that God had to teach his people that in his kingdom there was no room for this Jew/Gentile divide. Early on the Hebraic Jews discriminated even against the Greek speaking Jews. But there were only sinners, sinners that needed to be redeemed and sinners that had been redeemed by the blood of Jesus. The gospel was first preached to the gentiles in Antioch and it was where we were first called Christians. That city of about ½ million people was one of the four largest cities in the Roman Empire and was so depraved that at a later stage one Roman general would not let his troops enter the city when on leave. It was a centre of sex tourism based on the worship of Daphne and the city gave rise to the expression of the time, "the morals of Daphne." (Barclay, Ambassador for Christ p.64). The Roman poet Juvenal saw Antioch as a sewer discharging its corrupting influences into Rome (Satire 3:63). In this environment God showed his saving love for sinners. From this impossible soil grew the gentile church, our church. Our father was not seeking a group of people who could claim their own righteousness through obeying rules and separating themselves but who responded to the message of repentance and faith in the righteous crucified saviour.

A few years later, on Paul's second missionary trip he travelled from respectable Athens where there was little response and went to the then capital, Corinth. It was one of the largest cities in the empire. This was another city so renowned for immorality that the term "corinthianize" was a euphemism for loose living. When a Corinthian was shown in a Greek play he was always a drunk. There is a well known comment in by the geographer Strabo, *"And the temple of Aphrodite was so rich that it owned more than a thousand temple slaves, courtesans, whom both men and women had dedicated to the goddess."*[1] Well that was classical Greece but in Paul's time it was a Roman colony but still a place you went to enjoy sin. Based on the number there were in Rome, the number had grown to many times that. At the point of giving up when the Jews rejected the gospel, the Lord appeared to him in a vision telling him, "I have many people in this city" (Acts 18:10). Of course our faith encompasses the respectable and moral but in our respectability we can lose vision of a loving saviour and a

---

1 Strabo – Geographica – Book 8, Chapter 6

gospel with power to save sinners and the rejoicing in heaven when sinners repent.

## Point 2. A gospel that is still powerful for today's needs

His book contains accurate details of 1$^{st}$ century society, specifically with regard to titles of officials, administrative divisions, town assemblies and rules of the Jewish temple in Jerusalem. An example of its historical precision can be seen in Acts 14:6. There Luke implies that Iconium was not in Lycaonia while contemporary Romans such as Cicero said it was. Archaeologists claimed Acts to be unreliable until in 1910 when William Ramsay found evidence that Iconium was in Phrygia. "You may press the words of Luke," wrote Ramsay, "in a degree beyond any other historian's, and they stand the keenest scrutiny and the hardest treatment...."[2] This accuracy could not be achieved in the second century when many critics thought the book was written. But let's be perfectly honest, this historical precision of Acts is hand in hand with the description of a Christian experience far removed from our own. It is so different that it can leave unbelievers thinking it is nothing more than a fairy tale and believers despairing at the poverty of our own church age. Sir Robert Anderson, in his great book, *The Silence of God* said, "The mystery remains that God who at sundry times and in diverse manners spake in time past unto the fathers never speaks to his people now! The divine history of the favoured race for thousands of years teems with miracles by which God gave proof of his power with men, and yet we are confronted with the astonishing fact that from the days of the apostles to the present hour, the history of Christendom will be searched in vain for the record of a single public event to compel belief that there is a God at all!"

---

2 William M. Ramsay. The Bearing of Recent Discovery on the Trustworthiness of the New Testament (London: Hodder and Stroughton, 1915) p. 8

And yet, despite that being the reality that we older believers grew up with and some of us may have drummed into us as normal, we knew and still know the consolation of faith and the intimacy of the promised comforter who walks with us. But not just with us but who also went ahead plotting a path through fair wind and foul. Fortunately for the younger ones among us, the Australian believers need no longer experience God's silence. By 1995, church statisticians for the National Church Life Survey (NCLS) concluded encounters with God's power had become "a part of the faith journey of the majority of believers"[3]. The NCLS data showed that there was a stronger experience to answered prayer and the miraculous in faith communities that strongly encouraged their members to seek for them. I thank God that this is a community where we are encouraged to bring our needs before almighty God. Drew led us in prayer earlier and we are blessed to have Annette and he among us. I know of no one else's prayers that draw us before the throne of our father in such a way. It is a very precious gift. But whoever is praying, it is never just as empty words that might make us feel better inside but not change anything. Instead, it is done with expectancy that there is a loving saviour and friend who hears and answers.

Next book – Testimonies from a Potato Field?

**Point 3. Acts is a book whose end is at the beginning.**

Have you ever been reading a book and flicked to the back page to see how it ends? It's pretty common. In fact, the dearest page for advertising in a magazine is the outside of the back page. In his Gospel, Luke wrote about all that Jesus began to do and to teach and, in his second book, he wrote about what the apostles began to do and teach. The last chapter of the book of Acts ends with Paul

---

3Kaldor, Peter, Robert Dixon, Ruth Powel and the NCLS Team, *Taking Stock, a profile of Australian Church Attenders.* (Adelaide: Openbook Publishers, 1999) 88.

imprisoned in Rome. But that is not the last word. At the very beginning we are told the end:

*10 They were looking intently up into the sky as he was going, when suddenly two men dressed in white stood beside them. 11 "Men of Galilee," they said, "why do you stand here looking into the sky? This same Jesus, who has been taken from you into heaven, will come back in the same way you have seen him go into heaven."*

Stephen, as he was being stoned gazed into heaven and saw this same Jesus whom he called by his end time title, the Son of Man, standing at the right hand of God (Acts 7;55-6) and he saw the heavens opened. In a similar manner it appeared that, at times, my own mother gazed into heaven and urged us to praise him. The message preached had at its core judgement and the hope of the resurrection. History will not roll on forever and there is coming a time when the tribulations of this world will cease and we will see Jesus descending in like manner to the way he left. Not in that half way state between life and death, and not with the eyes of faith but with clarity and certainty we will see the resurrected Lord with our very eyes and we will meet him in the air.

The apostles wanted to know when this would be. They were impatient with the present and wanted to seize the future. Instead, Jesus diverts their attention from the future to the present, at which point the church much preach the gospel at home and at the uttermost parts of the earth. We look at events unfolding in the Middle East and ask, "Is this the time you are going to restore the kingdom?" The answer comes back, "It is not for you to know the times or dates the Father has set by his own authority." We can be so consumed with the mission of the church to seek and save the lost that we substitute it totally for seeking and praying for our Lord's return. We can be so content with the leading of the Holy Spirit that we no longer long for the presence of Jesus. We can easily forget that the church preaches and baptizes to prepare a people to meet the returning Christ. The early church had as its watchwords "Thy kingdom come" and "Maranatha"[4]. May it become ours as well.

## Conclusion

So, Acts, an old book about long dead people and cities, many of which have all but disappeared from the face of the earth, with cultures that are very different to ours. Yet for all that it deals with matters that are completely up to date. The clothing may be finer and the streets less dusty but all are still equally in need of a saviour. Its power to save sinners has not been diminished.

With our prosperity at one end and the welfare state at the other, combined with the wonders of modern science and medicine all lull many into a false security that they have no need of a Heavenly Father to direct their path and of the Holy Spirit to guide them into all truth. But for those who have tasted the friendship of the Lord and his mercy cannot conceive of a life where our every need is provided by him and who delights in answering our prayers.

Finally, for all its permanence, this world will pass away and we, just like those privileged disciples 2000 years ago who saw Jesus depart, will see our Lord return.

Maranatha. .

---

4 This is the Greek transliteration of two Aramaic words found once in both the New Testament in 1 Corinthians 16:22 and also in the Didache (10.6). Depending where the break is put it can either mean "our Lord has come" or "our Lord come."

# 2 WHEN LIFE INTERRUPTS OUR PLANS

*This sermon on the First Chapter of Ruth was preached a year after the next chapter of this book which is on Chapter Two of Ruth. It's content was prompted by the continuing and devastating drought that was crippling our valley, so soon after the Millennial Drought and the devastating floods of 2011. I had started on my commentary on Ruth which gave me background for the sermon. The sermon was delivered at Gatton Church of Christ, not Tenthill.*

[1] In the days when the judges judged, there was a famine in the land. A certain man of Bethlehem, Judah went to live in the country of Moab with his wife and his two sons. [2] The name of the man was Elimelech, and the name of his wife, Naomi. The names of his two sons were Mahlon and Chilion, Ephrathites of Bethlehem, Judah. They came into the country of Moab and lived there. [3] Elimelech, Naomi's husband, died and she was left with her two sons. [4] They took for themselves wives of the women of Moab. The name of the one was Orpah, and the name of the other was Ruth. They lived there about ten years. [5] Mahlon and Chilion both died, and the woman was bereaved of her two children and of her husband. [6] Then she arose with her daughters-in-law, that she might return from the country of Moab for she had heard in the country of Moab how Yahweh had visited his people in giving them bread. [7] She went out of the place where she was, and her two daughters-in-law with her. They went on the way to return to the land of Judah. [8] Naomi said to her two daughters-in-law, "Go, return each of you to her mother's house. May Yahweh deal kindly with you, as you have dealt with the dead and with me. [9] May Yahweh grant you that you may find rest, each of you in the house of her husband."

Then she kissed them, and they lifted up their voices, and wept. [10] They said to her, "No, but we will return with you to your people."

[11] Naomi said, "Go back, my daughters. Why do you want

to go with me? Do I still have sons in my womb, that they may be your husbands? [12] Go back, my daughters, go your way; for I am too old to have a husband. If I should say, 'I have hope,' if I should even have a husband tonight, and should also bear sons, [13] would you then wait until they were grown? Would you then refrain from having husbands? No, my daughters, for it grieves me seriously for your sakes, for Yahweh's hand has gone out against me."

[14] They lifted up their voices and wept again; then Orpah kissed her mother-in-law, but Ruth stayed with her. [15] She said, "Behold,[‡] your sister-in-law has gone back to her people and to her god. Follow your sister-in-law."

[16] Ruth said, "Don't urge me to leave you, and to return from following you, for where you go, I will go; and where you stay, I will stay. Your people will be my people, and your God[‡] my God. [17] Where you die, I will die, and there I will be buried. May Yahweh do so to me, and more also, if anything but death parts you and me."

[18] When Naomi saw that she was determined to go with her, she stopped urging her.

[19] So they both went until they came to Bethlehem. When they had come to Bethlehem, all the city was excited about them, and they asked, "Is this Naomi?"
[20] She said to them, "Don't call me Naomi.[§] Call me Mara,[*] for the Almighty has dealt very bitterly with me. [21] I went out full, and Yahweh has brought me home again empty. Why do you call me Naomi, since Yahweh has testified against me, and the Almighty has afflicted me?" [22] So Naomi returned, and Ruth the Moabitess, her daughter-in-law, with her, who returned out of the country of Moab. They came to Bethlehem in the beginning of barley harvest. (World English Bible Translation)

There is a saying, "Life is what happens to you when you are busy making other plans" and you are hard pressed to find a better example than that which is spread before us in Chapter 1 of Ruth. I must confess that my favourite book in the Bible is this very short story of Ruth the Moabitess. I say "confess" because, if I was a more spiritual man, I suppose it should be the gospels, or the exciting story of the early church or the deep theology of Romans but, none the less, it is Ruth. Make no mistake, I love Jesus and the message of the cross, but the gospels with their rising of the dead and the blind seeing is a world away for from my life experience. Likewise, with Acts with the added dimension of a world that was receptive to the gospel. Similarly, I can't associate with the palaces and wars of the Old Testament. But Ruth is another matter. In this little book we have country people living in a small town and dealing, as best they can, with what the Lord throws at them. Some do it well, others do it badly and some you can't be sure.

The promised land was called "a land flowing with milk and honey", but when you compare the rocky, hilly land around Bethlehem with our own fertile valley it is as if the Good Lord has a sense of humour. The land seemed barely marginal. It failed Abraham and he had to go to Egypt where he didn't pour glory on himself. It later failed Isaac and he was thinking of going to Egypt until the Lord appeared to him and said not to (Gen 26;2-5). Instead, he received a miraculous harvest right there in Canaan. It failed Jacob and the Lord miraculously prepared the deliverance of the family through Joseph in Egypt, not Canaan. Moses had told the children of Israel that the health of the land would be dependent on the spiritual health of the people (Deut 28) and, during the time of the judges, it was not good. The harvest had failed and there was famine in the land and the good were suffering equally with those who had forsaken the Lord.

I have a very good friend in Ethiopia who did his PhD at the Gatton University. We were in drought all the time he was here, and our valley opened his eyes. In his country, miss the rains and thousands starve, but here we just started up the pumps. We have no concept of what it is like to live on a knife-edge, one rainfall away from hunger and destitution. Yet this is what was thrown at Elimelek and Naomi and their two sons Mahlon and Kilion. No doubt the parent's plans for life were to live to a ripe old age, marry their sons to good Jewish girls who would have provided them with Jewish grandchildren. But, as the saying goes, "Life is what happens to you when you are busy making other plans."

There was no heavenly messenger commanding them to stay in Canaan and no supernatural harvest, just desperation and despair. So, with pain in their bellies, or at least its imminent threat, they packed up and moved to a land where their culture, their language and even their lineage were very similar, but it was also a land where the people worshipped Chemosh, a different god,. Never in their wildest imagination would they have contemplated such a move. For all their worship and faithfulness to the Lord they were faced with famine and had to find survival among a people whose religious practices the Lord called an abomination (1 Ki 11:7).

At that time, Midian was a land where there was no famine and their prosperity was attributed to the blessing of a vile god. What would this family have thought? Perhaps they asked, "What is the value in serving the Lord when those who don't are doing better." The wandering in the wilderness and the conquest of the land was not that many years behind them, remember that the mother of Boaz from Chapter Two of our book was Rahab from the destruction of Jericho. Naomi and Elimelek would have heard the stories and known old men who had seen and been part of the powerful things the Lord had done for Israel. There were too many witnesses to doubt it, and now this family from a new generation must have questioned why the Lord appeared to no longer go before them as before.

There are many who were found in a house of worship who have asked the same question and could not find an answer. My dear friends, some of you have lived longer than me. What has been your life journey? While I sincerely hope that hunger and deprivation was never a part of it, I expect that for some of you, life was what happened to your well-made plans. Despite disappointments, you are still found in a house of worship every Sunday. You have trust and have faith in a God who says he is merciful, and kind. A firm confidence in his nature and his promises is something you have been able to hold resolutely to, and we all must hold on to, despite the circumstances. "Thou wilt whisper Thy peace to my soul," as the hymnwriter says and what a blessing it is to know this.

While our story starts with a departure, one of the key words throughout this book is "return". Circumstances were largely out of the control of this family but what they could control they did, they did not abandon their faith in this foreign land, nor did they burn their bridges by selling the farm. Their time in Midian was never intended to be permanent nor was it intended to be their home. That farm was a visible sign that the God they served was a delivering God. Through Moses, the Lord had humiliated the gods of Egypt and delivered a nation of slaves through the Red Sea. He had delivered them by feeding and watering them for 40 years in the wilderness. Through Joshua that they had crossed the Jordan on dry ground, the walls of Jericho had fallen, and they had largely conquered the land. That plot of ground had come probably to Elimelek's father as the Lord's gift through the casting of lots. While the present situation didn't seem to line up with their delivering God, by retaining the plot Elimelek and Naomi were saying that ultimately, "Our deliverer can be trusted." Because of this family's trust and faithfulness, we have come to see deliverance in a much broader way, through the later Joshua, who we know as Jesus, who reconciled man and God. My friends as

Christians we also must consider where our home truly is, and this blessed valley isn't it.

The names used in this book are like an allegory. At the beginning, Naomi is described as being an Ephrathite of Bethlehem Judah. Ephrath was most likely the old Canaanite name for Bethlehem. It means "fruitful" while Bethlehem means "house of bread." The famine at the beginning of the story was a mockery of their hometown's names. But after ten years things were changing and very pointedly we are told in verse 6 that the Lord had attended to his people by giving them "bread". The play on words continues when in her despair Naomi says [20] "Don't call me Naomi," she told them. "Call me Mara, because the Almighty has made my life very bitter. [21] I went away full, but the LORD has brought me back empty. Why call me Naomi? The LORD has afflicted me; the Almighty has brought misfortune upon me."

Naomi, what is in a name? It is most likely an abbreviated name that means "God is sweet," or, literally, "Jah is sweetness." It had very likely been given to her by her grateful and happy parents that had been led to think that "sweet are the ways, sweet are the dealings, and sweet is the character of God." She now saw the name she was given and the hopes for her life and a statement about the God of Israel as a mockery of the fate inflicted upon her. She asks instead that she should be called by a new name, *Mara* meaning "bitter". Her language is similar to that of Job and suggests but is ambiguous as to whether she sees herself suffering unjustly but she did suffer without explanation.

We could start to get all morbid here, and our story is sad, it is tragic but only if we let their journey of faith stay in Chapter One. Like Job, Naomi also will be restored when any hope of restoration seems impossible. The family did not know about the sorrow that awaited them in Midian and they certainly did not know about the joy and restoration in Chapter Four that would ultimately bless all mankind. Sadness and sorrow will probably be the lot of all of us at some stage. That is life, and it is what happens to our plans, but bitterness of spirit is a different matter. It is a disease that is hard to cure but in her case the remedy was staring her in the face; her two daughters-in-law who loved her more than life itself.

You have heard the story of the man on the rooftop during a flood. The SES comes by, but he won't get in the boat. "God is going to save me," he says. Soon after the rescue helicopter comes by. Again he refuses help because God is going to save him. A third time, the SES comes back and the same story. The floods rise and he drowns and standing before the throne he asks, "God, why didn't you save me." To which the Lord said, "I tried three times."

Her daughters-in-law showed her the "loving kindness" that she was looking to God for. Naomi said, "May the Lord show you kindness, as you have shown kindness to your dead husbands and to me." That word kindness is a term that is extraordinarily difficult to translate into English. Our language has no obvious equivalent. Many books have been written about it trying to get some understanding of this word, Hesed, which is found almost 250 times in the Old Testament. One book I read on the word described the core meaning of the word as

- The person who gives *hesed* is recognised as having a responsibility to the recipient,
- The giver is free not to perform *hesed*.
- The act fulfils an important need for the recipient; and
- Only the giver is in the position to help

This "loving kindness" appears to be part of the very character of God and you can see this in verses such as Psalm 62:12, "To Thee, Oh Lord belongs steadfast love", and also in Psalm 109:21, "But you, Sovereign Lord, help me for your name's sake; out of the goodness of your love, deliver me." And again in 25:10ff "All the ways of the Lord are loving and faithful toward those who keep the demands of his covenant." One writer described this love Naomi received from her daughters-in-law this way "It is not a human achievement but a quality we know from God, a quality man is expected to emulate." God's hesed is better than life, (Psm. 63:3), and lasts forever, (Psm. 136). "Where is your loving kindness?" Naomi asked and her God said nothing, But Ruth, her daughter-in-law, replied, "Don't urge me to leave you or to turn back from you. Where you go I will go, and where you stay I will stay. Your people will be my people and your God my God. [17] Where you die I will die, and there I will be buried. May the LORD deal with me, be it ever so severely, if even death separates you and me."

There was no voice from heaven but instead two daughters-in-law who would rather face a life of poverty helping their mother-in-law than to find security in the home of another husband. Likewise, our Lord's provision will be at hand for you. There is no place and no need for a bitter spirit before him.

On that road so long ago, God showed that he was faithful. Naomi's parents' belief that "sweet are the ways, sweet are the dealings, and sweet is the character of God" was not misplaced. Naomi may have been slow on the uptake, as we too often are, even when God's provision and love are staring us in the face. I am not far from 70 years old. A lot of life has happened to my plans, and yes there has been a lot of disappointment and sadness and questioning. What about you? Knowing all this, will you still not agree with me that our Lord was never far from us, that his deliverance, often from the most unlikely of sources was always at hand. Would you not agree with me today that sweet are our Lord's ways, sweet are his dealings, and sweet is his character?

# 3 RUTH GLEANS AT BOAZ'S FIELD

*In the absence of a senior pastor, our youth pastor, Tim Grant, rose to the challenge. He grew in his abilities as the lord equipped him for the new role. This sermon is part of a series he gave on Ruth. I was given the task of preaching on Chapter 2 up to verse 12. Ruth is my favourite book in the Bible.*

**Reading:** Ruth Meets Boaz in the Grain Field

[1] Naomi had a relative of her husband's, a mighty man of wealth, of the family of Elimelech, and his name was Boaz. [2] Ruth the Moabitess said to Naomi, "Let me now go to the field, and glean among the ears of grain after him in whose sight I find favor."

She said to her, "Go, my daughter." [3] She went, and came and gleaned in the field after the reapers; and she happened to come to the portion of the field belonging to Boaz, who was of the family of Elimelech.

[4] Behold, Boaz came from Bethlehem, and said to the reapers, "May Yahweh be with you."

They answered him, "May Yahweh bless you."

[5] Then Boaz said to his servant who was set over the reapers, "Whose young lady is this?"

[6] The servant who was set over the reapers answered, "It is the Moabite lady who came back with Naomi out of the country of Moab. [7] She said, 'Please let me glean and gather after the reapers among the sheaves.' So she came, and has continued even from the morning until now, except that she rested a little in the house."

[8] Then Boaz said to Ruth, "Listen, my daughter. Don't go to glean in another field, and don't go from here, but stay here close to my maidens. [9] Let your eyes be on the field that they reap, and go after

them. Haven't I commanded the young men not to touch you? When you are thirsty, go to the vessels, and drink from that which the young men have drawn."

[10] Then she fell on her face and bowed herself to the ground, and said to him, "Why have I found favor in your sight, that you should take knowledge of me, since I am a foreigner?"

[11] Boaz answered her, "I have been told all about what you have done for your mother-in-law since the death of your husband, and how you have left your father, your mother, and the land of your birth, and have come to a people that you didn't know before. [12] May Yahweh repay your work, and a full reward be given to you from Yahweh, the God of Israel, under whose wings you have come to take refuge." World English Translation

Ruth 2:10 At this she bowed down with her face to the ground. She asked him, "Why have I found such favor in your eyes that you notice me—a foreigner?"

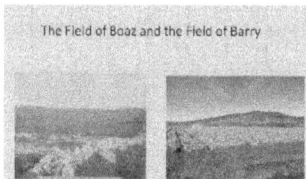

**Text:** 2:10 At this she bowed down with her face to the ground. She asked him, "Why have I found such favor in your eyes that you notice me—a foreigner?"

The Field of Boaz and the Field of Barry

Each Sunday, we look out at Barry and Leone's farm, a farm that Wikipedia says is part of the third most fertile soil in the world. When I do, I can't help thinking, at times, that the Good Lord had a sense of humour. You see, he described the Promised Land as a land flowing with milk and honey. Yet, this is the land that failed Abraham and he had to go to Egypt to survive, in another drought

Isaac seriously considered the same thing but was saved by a supernatural harvest, again Jacob and his 70 family members had to go to Egypt because of another drought and now, yet again, the land is recovering, this time from a 10-year drought. We know about 10-year droughts don't we! To us, the rocky land without irrigation looks barely marginal and the Biblical record shows that life could be lived on a knife edge. In a land and time where every head of wheat could count, the Good Lord said in Leviticus 19:9-10 9

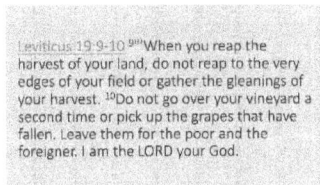

Leviticus 19:9-10 9'' When you reap the harvest of your land, do not reap to the very edges of your field or gather the gleanings of your harvest. 10 Do not go over your vineyard a second time or pick up the grapes that have fallen. Leave them for the poor and the foreigner. I am the LORD your God.

'"When you reap the harvest of your land, do not reap to the very edges of your field or gather the gleanings of your harvest. [10]Do not go over your vineyard a second time or pick up the grapes that have fallen. Leave them for the poor and the foreigner. I am the LORD your God.

Here the individual sheaves have been put together into a stook

Perhaps it is good to have a reminder of not so ancient harvesting practices, It is not so ancient because the combine harvester only dates to 1885. Before that traditional hand-reapers, using sickles or scythes and, working as a team, usually cut a field of grain clockwise, starting from an outside edge and finishing in the middle. Scything would therefore leave a windrow of cut stems to the left of the reaper and, if cut skilfully, leave the seed heads more or less aligned. These are then picked up and tied into sheaves by following workers using other cut stems as ties. These workers, or a following team, would  then stand the sheaves up in stooks to dry.  This all left room for a wastage of grain.

Harvesting in the Field of Boaz Near Bethlehem

We are told that in surrounding cultures there were similar gleaning laws to help the poor but only in Israel did the law extend to the foreigner.  Helping close relatives, yes, helping members of the same clan, or the same tribe, yes, members of the same covenant, yes.  But helping a poor foreigner where there is neither the slightest obligation nor chance of repayment, that is another matter.  It makes no sense in a land where crops were poor by modern standards and harvesting inefficient, to make it less so.  But as one writer says, "We might classify gleaning as an expression of compassion or justice, but according to Leviticus, allowing others to glean on our property is the fruit of holiness. We do it because God says, "I am the Lord your God."

1910 postcard of Boaz's field – notice the rock

These words, *I am the Lord your God,* are the preamble to the Ten Commandments, the covenant between the Lord and Israel.  Here in this and other passages from Leviticus they were most likely shorthand for the covenant.  The farmer who did not harvest up to the boundary was saying, "I may never see God's mighty hand in this life like my forefathers, (but writing my book of Tenthill testimonies has taught me one thing, some of you surely have,) but even if not, I remember where I have come from."  It was a reminder that, with a mighty hand, they were bought out of Egypt, out of the house of bondage.  There was no rule about how much of the edge of your field you didn't harvest and the moment you did make a rule, it ceased to be a spiritual exercise. To not harvest right up to edges of the field was an acknowledgement that God is not always busy elsewhere. The old Scottish saying which was common when I was young was "Many a mickle makes a muckle" but this law about harvesting was saying your prosperity does not come from frugality but from God's blessing on your generosity.

Modern view of the Field of Boaz Near Bethlehem

The right to glean the edges of the field was not just given by the Almighty to the righteous who were worthy of our support but to the unrighteous as well. A judgemental and critical spirit is the risk of Christians who claim to be trophies of grace. The providences of God in a fallen world can sometimes appear harsh and the attitude can easily be, "Who sinned." By relieving their suffering am I working against some divine and just dispensation and we certainly see that in India under the caste system. It is easy to say that this act, or that circumstance of their own making, caused their poverty. And sometimes that is right; they made their own bed and now they can lie in it. I dare say that this judgemental attitude is not far from any one of us. But the God who sent droughts on sinners is also the same God who also sent manna to the wilful and disobedient children of Israel in the wilderness and who still sends his rain on the just and unjust. Our own experience of droughts that fall upon the righteous should cause us never to be judgmental of the circumstances of others for in doing so we judge ourselves. May our mercy never, ever be conditional.

Leviticus 19:31-34 "The stranger who resides with you shall be to you as the native among you, and you shall love him as yourself, for you were aliens in the land of Egypt; I am the LORD your God."

Further, Leviticus 19:31-34 says "The stranger who resides with you shall be to you as the native among you, and you shall love him as yourself, for you were aliens in the land of Egypt; I am the LORD your God."

The foreigner you will love as yourself

How do we see this command to love foreigners worked out here in this field near Bethlehem? I am grateful to a Jewish commentator for her insight. You see, the overseer has a lot to say to Boaz and it is all critical. He told him that Ruth is a Moabite, hinting that she does not really belong there. By changing just one word in her request—she asked for permission to glean from the sheaves, he says she asked permission to glean from the stalks, something she had no right to do. This makes her sound greedy and presumptuous, without directly saying so. Then he says that Ruth has been standing since the morning. Gleaners do not stand; they move. They follow the harvesters, they sit and they glean. Why, then, does the overseer say that Ruth has been standing all day? Perhaps he is hinting that he ordered her to stand and wait until the master arrives and decides whether to give her permission to glean or not. In three brief sentences, the overseer has put Ruth down, and has shown off his own ability to keep unworthy strangers out—without quite saying a single explicitly negative word about her. This Jewish commentator says we should "learn to see the overseer as a bigot who dislikes strangers." To which I would add, it is a big deal to not let her drink from the water jars and that, above everything, shows what was going on here.

Harvesting in the field of Boaz near Bethlehem

An old man, and an attractive young woman, and a workplace where the proprietary of the younger men couldn't automatically be guaranteed is prime ground for some very unsavoury comments. And I think we can say that she was attractive as Boaz sees an expression of her noble character in that she "not run after the younger men, whether rich or poor." Over recent years we have become aware that a safe workplace is much more than just guarding our machines. We must also be diligent now that the correct wages are being paid by the contractors we engage. Stories that have come out of recent years of underpayment in a wide range of industries have been shameful. Perhaps more shameful has been the disclosure of sexual harassment of workers from back packers all the way up to high profile actresses.

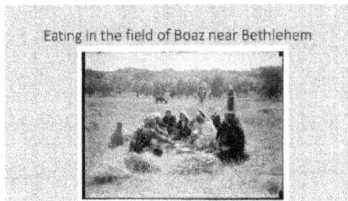

Eating in the field of Boaz near Bethlehem

When he came to the field, Boaz said, "The LORD be with you!" "The LORD bless you!" they answered. The words were right, but Boaz didn't let that blind him to human nature, especially in a workplace where you would expect the atmosphere to be set by the overseer. Before he even met Ruth, Boaz warned the young men – leave her alone, keep your hands off her. And later for her own safety he advises Ruth don't glean in anyone else's field. Some of you may have a sexual harassment policy in place and employees may have to acknowledge it but going from words to practice requires diligence. This is the fruit of holiness, not a begrudging compliance to government workplace regulations.

Ruth had no idea what she was going to expect that day. "Let me go to the fields and pick up the leftover grain behind anyone in whose eyes I find favor." The word for favour is one of three Hebrew words that make up our understanding of grace. Tim introduced us to one of these three last week, Hesed, covenant responsibility. It's a key word in understanding the book of Ruth. The root of our word today, which is found in verse 2 and 10 and next week in verse 13, "depicts a heartfelt response by someone who has something to give to one who has a need". That is more than charity and it is much more than obligation. She didn't find grace and favour with the overseer and she must have been disappointed and wondering if she had made a good choice going to that field. But Boaz sees right through his overseer and goes over to Ruth and is gracious to her, addressing her in the most tender way "My daughter". Without knowing her, he was gracious to her ensuring her safety at work but now he does he goes further and blesses this foreigner, who until a few days beforehand had followed idols.

Winnowed grain in Bethlehem

Strictly, Boaz doesn't bless her. He blessed his workers when he arrived but here he is more thoughtful. [12] May the LORD repay you for what you have done. May you be richly rewarded by the LORD, the God of Israel, under whose wings you have come to take refuge." The enormity of what she has done, leaving her security for what can only be expected to be poverty and hardship because of her love for her mother-in-law is not lost on this man of substance. In coming weeks, we will see that the vague prayer for blessing is given real substance as he goes out and does for Ruth with his own hands the request he has sent up to the heavens. But that is months away in Ruth's life and the wedding is not in anyone's mind yet, he was just a gracious old man who was kind to one of his relatives. But do you notice, even now the very thing Boaz asked God to do, he does himself. He will make sure that she does not go home empty handed, hungry and thirsty.

Where is God in all of this? There are no visions, no dreams, no angels, no voices from heaven, no miracles but the Almighty's hand is at work. And it is at work in the same way as we know it here in this farming community and can see it clearly through the vision of faith. God has blessed Boaz with a productive farm and he was fully aware of God's role in his labour, because he repeatedly invoked the Lord's blessing (Ruth 2:4; 3:10). But don't think for one moment that Boaz's possession of this land was his through astute business practices or better farming. It came to his father by casting of a lot, the throw of a dice, after the conquest. Another Judean we see in Judges 15 complained that she had been allocated desert and asked for a spring. Ruth just happened to come upon Boaz's field. The odd construction of "her chance chanced upon" in Ruth 2:3 is deliberate. "In colloquial English, we would say, "As her luck would have it." But the statement is ironic. The writer intentionally uses an expression that forces the reader to sit up and ask how it could be that Ruth "happened" to land in the field of a man who was not only gracious but also a kinsman. As the story unfolds, we see that Ruth's arrival at Boaz' field was evidence of God's providential hand. The same can be said for the appearance of the next-of-kin just as Boaz sat down at the gate."

The overseer sums up what was wrong with Israel in the time when everybody did what was right in their own eyes, but the story shifts quickly to the exemplary behaviour of Ruth and Boaz. These two through small acts of kindness and humanity would change the course of history and restore hope and unity to a nation. None of us here are going to be forefathers and mothers of the saviour of the world but does our heavenly father care for you any less? Does he order the circumstances of your life any the less? But in the throw of the dice that is called life never forget that it is the Lord himself who throws them, and we have been blessed with extraordinary blessings.

Can you imagine being at the reading of the will and the solicitor says, "To my first-born son, I leave the family farm, 300 acres in down town Ropely." It's only one valley over but, as old Arnie Schultz5 said, "When it rained for 40 days and 40 nights, we got 40 points in Ropely." Great if there was a booming market for goannas. (Who among us would say that the old Lutheran farmers in the next valley loved the Lord less than us.) The good fortune that came our way places an enormous responsibility on us to live a life that is the fruit of holiness. For some, this blessing is just being able to live in peace in the best part of a prosperous nation. For some, this good fortune came through inheritance, some through ability, skill and hard work. For others, it is the blessing of having a safety net provided by a nation that once drew its values from the gospel. Not one of us can say that God was busy elsewhere. Look how little it took to turn an act from charity to one of grace and holiness and inclusion. It was only a kind word, a safe work place, a drink of water and a shared meal. Every one of us is capable of doing this. It quickly culminated in two lives becoming one and lived in faithfulness to each other and lived also in the presence of the LORD, the God of Israel, under whose wings they have come to take refuge.

Go thou and do likewise because we too shelter under these same wings.

# 4. A CHURCH THAT KNOWS THE GOSPEL

*Tim was doing a series of sermons entitled The Nine Signs of a Healthy Church. I was given the third sign, A Church that Knows the Gospel. A visitor to the valley on business was driving past and was compelled to come in. I trust he had an appointment with the gospel.*

**Reading: 1 Cor. 15:1-11**

**Text: Gal. 16:6-9** I am astonished that you are so quickly deserting the one who called you to live in the grace of Christ and are turning to a different gospel— 7 which is really no gospel at all. Evidently some people are throwing you into confusion and are trying to pervert the gospel of Christ. 8 But even if we or an angel from heaven should preach a gospel other than the one we preached to you, let them be under God's curse! 9 As we have already said, so now I say again: If anybody is preaching to you a gospel other than what you accepted, let them be under God's curse!

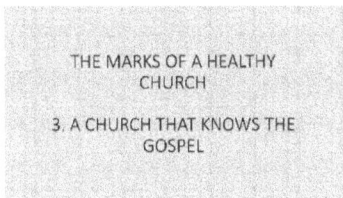

THE MARKS OF A HEALTHY CHURCH

3. A CHURCH THAT KNOWS THE GOSPEL

We are working through a series entitled the nine signs of a healthy church and we are up to number three, A church that knows the gospel.

I have heard it said, "Blonds have more fun"

LEGALLY blonde

Well, it's said that blondes have more fun. I really can't say about that, but three Sundays ago, when I was walking in Melbourne, I thought, for a brief moment, that the Collins Street Baptists at least might have more fun, blonde or otherwise.

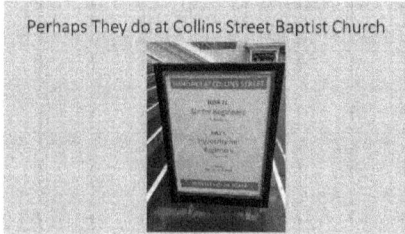

Perhaps They do at Collins Street Baptist Church

You see, I noticed this sign outside of their church that was advertising upcoming sermon titles. "Sinning for beginners" and "Hypocrisy for beginners." Now, I fully expect, and certainly hope that these were just catchy titles to draw in passersby who would not normally attend, and it definitely made me look. But we are fooling ourselves if we think that there are not churches where the substance of these sermon titles has not been order of the day.

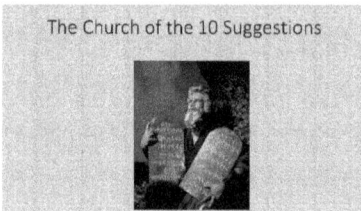

The Church of the 10 Suggestions

There are churches that accept every manner of God dishonouring practice as ones that should be embraced with pride. The church of the ten suggestions they may be termed. The findings of the royal commission have exposed masters of hypocrisy in our midst, not beginners. All of this has been done in name of the glorious gospel of Christ. By absorbing the character of a lost and sinful world instead of standing separate, they have, in their attempt to be inclusive, only seen more and more empty pews.

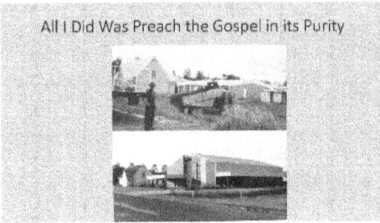

All I Did Was Preach the Gospel in its Purity

In the 1960's the Lutheran church in Gatton which met in the little wooden church on the corner of Spencer Street and East Street was reduced to a faithful few following a disastrous pastorate. They called eight pastors and none would come because of its past. In desperation, they called Pastor Len Mirtshin from the Ropely parish in 1963. That is very unusual. Our search committee didn't ring Doug5 and ask him if he was ready for a promotion. In about 1965 something happened. The church started to grow. They had to bring in extra chairs, and soon there were so many extra chairs that the only way to get out after the service was to remove chairs. It was an OH&S nightmare. So, they built a new hall and it filled and growth continued until about 1981. With only enough money for the foundations they started building the large church we now know, and the Lord provided every cent and all the volunteer labour to bring it to completion. I remember going there for school services and the deacons would walk up and down the aisles getting people to move along so more could fit in. Back then, we were so insular that we probably didn't notice, and we certainly didn't rejoice with them.

Pastor Mertshin was asked what was the key to this thing which was unprecedented in the history of the Lutheran church in Australia. His reply was, "I just preach the gospel in its truth and purity." To that should be added that it was also the time of God's visitation. Incidentally, from that slide does anyone remember Freddy Manteuffel? You don't find characters like that anymore.

---

5 The Gatton Baptist pastor.

What Does Gospel Mean?

Our English word Gospel is from Old English *gôdspell*, from *gôd* good + *spell* message; and is the translation of the Greek noun *euangelion* (occurring 76 times) "good news," and the verb *euangelizo*, (occurring 54 times), meaning "to bring or announce good news." Both words are derived from the noun angelos, "messenger."

The gospel in its purity and truth, but what is that? The word *Gospel* is old English meaning good news and was used to translate the New Testament word meaning just that. But what is this good news?

How Many Gospels Are There?

| | |
|---|---|
| Social gospel | Liberation theology gospel |
| Full gospel | Prosperity gospel |
| Four square gospel | Self Esteem gospel |
| Environmental gospel | Feminine gospel |

There are many contenders for that title and I put a few together. I have probably heard of many more, but I am getting a bit forgetful in my old age.

Social gospel
Liberation theology gospel
Full gospel
Prosperity gospel
Four square gospel
Self Esteem gospel
Environmental gospel
Feminine gospel

Fake News Folks

PRES TRUMP: FAKE NEWS IS THE ENEMY OF THE PEOPLE

As President Trump would say "Fake news, folks, and this fake news is definitely the enemy of the people. There is only "the gospel" which is meant to be preached in its purity and truth to all men and women, whether inside the church, whatever their faith tradition and to those outside. It doesn't need a descriptive word or term before it. But again, I say, what is it? How can you encapsulate in a few words when it takes a book to tell it? Just getting to the substance of it takes the first four chapters of Romans.

What is the Gospel?

Let me tell a story. On my first trip to the Philippines to speak at a conference, I travelled with a friend from Bible College and I met my evangelist friend, Fred Kornis, for the first time. My friend and Fred were doing some denomination bashing over their neglect of the gospel, and sadly we know there are times that it has been well deserved. I listened and finally added my two cents worth. I told them that I had observed that people who had been evangelicals would come to these very same denominations they had been criticising and say, "Will you now look after my parents for me in their old age." I commented that in the final washup we may find that our own gospel had been deficient.

Well, I am sure Fred who had probably been looking at me a bit suspiciously up to that point finally thought I had grown horns and asked, "And what is the gospel?" I really had to think. I could not put it in a few words. I started with the creation of a good and perfect world and of mankind who was in union with his maker. I told him of how sin entered, and mankind fell but that God had promised a saviour right from the beginning. I told him about a salvation history where the descendants of one man were brought into friendship with God and about how God taught them that he required a separated and holy life. I told him about the promised redeemer, our beloved Jesus, God's only son who was born as a babe and lived a perfect life and so showing us how we also should live. I told him how, as a young man he was crucified in my place, bearing my sin and died the death that my rebellion should have brought on me. I told Fred how, on the third day, he rose from the grave and how, completely by grace, he imparts his life through rebirth to all who will follow him in repentance and faith. With each sentence those imagined horns grew a little smaller and we would become very close friends and share in the work of the gospel.

While it satisfied Fred, it didn't satisfy me but not because it was wrong. I couldn't think of a single verse where the whole of the gospel is encapsulated, and I wanted a nice simple definition. I thought that this would be a good test for me to know whether I am keeping the main thing the main thing.

> ### What is the Gospel
>
> "The gracious promise of the forgiveness of sins for Christ's sake – this, and nothing but this is the gospel"

Reading the Lutheran theologian Herman Sasse one day, I found where he summarised Luther's rediscovery of the gospel which caused the Reformation, the fruits of which we all enjoy. Sasse used these words to define Luther's understanding of the gospel *"The gracious promise of the forgiveness of sins for Christ's sake – this, and nothing but this is the gospel"*. It jelled for me, the gospel in 11 words but try as I might I have not been able to find an original Luther quotation and, after last week, I dare not have an inaccurate one.6  But I can quote one of their confessions (FC SD, V, 20).

> ### What is the Gospel
>
> "The content of the Gospel is this, that the Son of God, Christ our Lord, himself assumed and bore the curse of the law and expiated and paid for all our sins, that through him alone we re-enter the good graces of God, obtain forgiveness of sins through faith, are freed from death and all the punishments of sin, and are saved eternally." from Formula of Concord

The content of the Gospel is this, that the Son of God, Christ our Lord, himself assumed and bore the curse of the law and expiated and paid for all our sins, that through him alone we re-enter the good graces of God, obtain forgiveness of sins through faith, are freed from death and all the punishments of sin, and are saved eternally.

So, do we want definitions and creeds, or do we want scripture? Think of these wonderful verses

**Ephesians 1:7**: In him we have redemption through his blood, the forgiveness of sins, in accordance with the riches of God's grace.

**Ephesians 2:8**: For it is by grace you have been saved, through faith--and this is not from yourselves, it is the gift of God.

**1 Cor 2:2**: I decided to know nothing among you except Jesus Christ and him crucified.

**Rom 1:16**: For I am not ashamed of the gospel, for it is the power of God for salvation to everyone who believes,

**Mark 10:45**: [Jesus] came to serve and give life as a ransom.

---

6 When preaching on the first sign, Pastor Tim gave a quotation from Luther which basically did was preach the word and the word did its work. I knew the quotation and in good humour corrected him as he had said all he did was preach the word, sleep and drink Wittenberg beer. We had an equally good humoured correction the week before.

These verses and others that we could think of all add a little bit extra into the mix in defining our understanding of the Gospel. Our scriptures, taken together lead to our definitions, and our definitions (and we will have them whether or not we have consciously written them down) help us give us a framework to interpret the scriptures. They are not mutually exclusive and are a guard against error.

For instance, when someone says that the gospel is simply that Jesus wants to be our friend we can confidentially say "No" because we know we have a past to deal with that could only be covered by grace and forgiveness. Should someone come and say, "The gospel is simply that God is love", you can say "No" because then you would not have needed Christ. But you can say, because he loved there is Christ. When we are tempted to say that the gospel has failed to run its course because we are so changeable, we can say with equal confidence "No" because the promises are God's not ours and he, at least, is unchangeable. The gracious promise of the forgiveness of sins for Christ's sake. In its simplicity the gospel is knowable by all.

> What of Repentance
>
> Not the labor of my hands
> Can fulfill Thy law's demands;
> Could my zeal no respite know,
> Could my tears forever flow,
> All for sin could not atone;
> Thou must save, and Thou alone

But what of my repentance and sorrow for my sin? The gospel isn't, do this, don't do that, avoid such and such, I want you to do this. An old friend who was a district commissioner in Tanganyika had a painting of his African cook on his wall. This weather beaten old cook was also the local Iman at the time. He had it there on his wall, he told me, because his cook was the most morally upright man he had ever met. A district commissioner with virtually the power of life and death and a lowly cook, but because of his upright life if he told the commissioner, you have offended such and such a person and he has lost face, he would go immediately and rectify matters. The heathen and the unbelievers can sometimes know more about moral living than a Christian, but it is only in the pages of this book that a person can learn of the gospel of grace and forgiveness. Repentance outside of grace is not salvation. The hymn, Rock of Ages, says it clearly.

Not the labour of my hands
Can fulfil Thy law's demands;
Could my zeal no respite know,
Could my tears forever flow,
All for sin could not atone;
Thou must save, and Thou alone

The gospel bids us stretch out our hand and receive. This time I will quote Luther correctly "Behold dear fellow, this has God done for thee, he gave his son to become flesh for thee, for thy sake allowed him to be slain." The only repentance that is acceptable to God is that which is a fruit of grace, never its means.

> What of Faith
>
> Are we, in one hand holding faith as "confidence in God's mercy, that he will be gracious for Christs sake, without any merit on my own part" and in the other turning faith into a work.

What of my faith? Christians look to Jesus as the saviour of sinners. They are told that because of their full and total forgiveness that they can come boldly before the throne of almighty God but many still retain how they previously knew him on an equal footing. They can still look to him as their lawgiver and teacher of morals. In one hand they can holding faith as "confidence in God's mercy, that he will be gracious for Christs sake, without any merit on my own part" and in the other faith is turned into a work. There is the world of difference between doing good deeds that arise naturally grateful transformed heart that wants to share that same grace he has received and doing it to receive grace.

Starting well and reverting to past ways has been a long-standing problem - Gal 3;1 You foolish Galatians! Who has bewitched you? Before your very eyes Jesus Christ was clearly portrayed as crucified. 2 I would like to learn just one thing from you: Did you receive the Spirit by the works of the law, or by believing what you heard? 3 Are you so foolish? After beginning by means of the Spirit, are you now trying to finish by means of the flesh? My faith and your faith by which we believed, even that was a gift of grace.

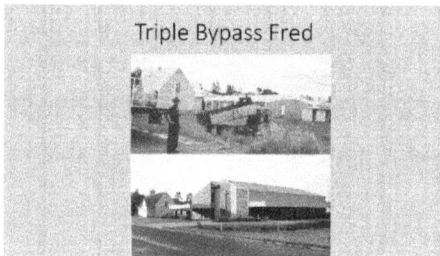

Triple Bypass Fred

What is the gospel? I have asked a few times and I ask it again, what is the gospel? Let's look at this image again. You can see Trevor Jackwitz's old truck when they started to filling the old swamp where Peace Lutheran Church now stands. In the foreground is Freddie Manteufel. In the latter part of his life Fred had earned the nickname, "Triple Bypass Fred." That wasn't referring to the number of coronary bypasses he had rather to the number of times he was at death's door and the Church prayed him back. I was talking to him shortly before he died, and he told me how, on the last occasion he had passed from this life into the next and had stood before the throne of God before being called back. He told me of his longing now to cast off this mortal coil and return to his true home.  This, my friends is the gospel.

Probably all of us have known a personal time of God's visitation where the truth of the gospel pierced our hearts.  If the Lord is speaking to you this morning, don't leave this place until the Gospel has done its work in you and you know the relief of your sins washed away and friendship with your maker.  Greg and I will remain at the front after the service for any who would like to start

into the well trodden path of faith and friendship with God.

# 5 THE PARABLE OF THE TRACTOR

*This communion address was prompted by one of our members, a farmer, who set me the challenge of working a tractor into a communion address.*

Parable of the Tractor

A few weeks back, Jason asked if I could work a tractor into a communion talk. Well why not. If our Lord could sit in a fishing boat and look out over the landscape and see a farmer going about his business of sowing seed and then give us the parable of the four soils it seems to be completely reasonable to draw some allusions from your everyday life. I think I am up to six possible lessons. If I get to 10, I might write a book.

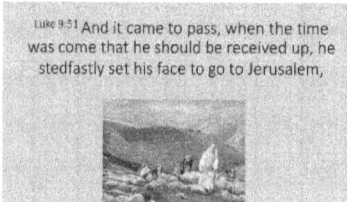

Luke 9:51 And it came to pass, when the time was come that he should be received up, he stedfastly set his face to go to Jerusalem,

Jesus set his face resolutely to go up to Jerusalem knowing full well what was waiting for him. He was unflinching and did not deviate from side to side in his purpose, the dreadful price of our redemption.

The other side of the cross is a long walk in the one direction

But my focus this morning is on the view past the cross and, what someone spoke to me about concerning our shared faith, what he called, "A long walk in the one direction." The cross behind us and before us that day when we will eat with our saviour in his kingdom. That brings us to the tractor.

Up till 1926 the Lanz Bulldog did not have reverse gear.

My lesson is drawn from the Lanz Bulldog which did not have reverse gear as standard until 1926! Consider how you would drive if your tractor did not have reverse gear! I think it would be very carefully. No easy backing up if you are not lined up perfectly with where the GPS wants you. Likewise, as we continue our walk in the one direction we should walk it very carefully and resolutely

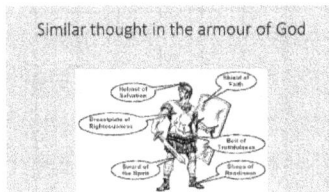
Similar thought in the armour of God

Paul, a prisoner of Rome, looked around at his circumstances and saw in the Roman soldiers that guarded him and drew another allusion, the armour of God. All given for protection when facing the enemy, none for retreat. The armour was our protection for our long walk in the one direction.

Father, give us the grace and courage that we may we be faithful to the end.

*Now obviously, even with the greatest care you eventually had to go backwards in your tractor. To achieve this, you got out of your seat, stopped the tractor and as the flywheel is rocking backwards and forwards before it everything was still, the operator gave the flywheel a quick flick backwards and the engine ran in backwards. Forward gears became reverse gears!*

.

# 6 LESSONS FROM THE EARLY CHURCH

This sermon was prompted by reading Peter Oakes' book, *Reading Romans in Pompeii, Paul's letter at Ground Level*

**Reading:** Rom 12

12 Therefore, I urge you, brothers and sisters, in view of God's mercy, to offer your bodies as a living sacrifice, holy and pleasing to God—this is your true and proper worship. [2] Do not conform to the pattern of this world, but be transformed by the renewing of your mind. Then you will be able to test and approve what God's will is—his good, pleasing and perfect will.

[3] For by the grace given me I say to every one of you: Do not think of yourself more highly than you ought, but rather think of yourself with sober judgment, in accordance with the faith God has distributed to each of you. [4] For just as each of us has one body with many members, and these members do not all have the same function, [5] so in Christ we, though many, form one body, and each member belongs to all the others. [6] We have different gifts, according to the grace given to each of us. If your gift is prophesying, then prophesy in accordance with your faith; [7] if it is serving, then serve; if it is teaching, then teach; [8] if it is to encourage, then give encouragement; if it is giving, then give generously; if it is to lead, do it diligently; if it is to show mercy, do it cheerfully.

[9] Love must be sincere. Hate what is evil; cling to what is good. [10] Be devoted to one another in love. Honor one another above yourselves. [11] Never be lacking in zeal, but keep your spiritual fervor, serving the Lord. [12] Be joyful in hope, patient in affliction, faithful in prayer. [13] Share with the Lord's people who are in need.

Practise hospitality.

[14] Bless those who persecute you; bless and do not curse. [15] Rejoice with those who rejoice; mourn with those who mourn. [16] Live in harmony with one another. Do not be proud, but be willing to associate with people of low position. Do not be conceited.

[17] Do not repay anyone evil for evil. Be careful to do what is right in the eyes of everyone. [18] If it is possible, as far as it depends on you, live at peace with everyone. [19] Do not take revenge, my dear friends, but leave room for God's wrath, for it is written: "It is mine to avenge; I will repay," says the Lord. [20] On the contrary:

"If your enemy is hungry, feed him;
If he is thirsty, give him something to drink.
In doing this, you will heap burning coals on his head."
[21] Do not be overcome by evil, but overcome evil with good."

**Text:** 12:1 Therefore, I urge you, brothers and sisters, in view of God's mercy, to offer your bodies as a living sacrifice, holy and pleasing to God—this is your true and proper worship. 2 Do not conform to the pattern of this world, but be transformed by the renewing of your mind. Then you will be able to test and approve what God's will is—his good, pleasing and perfect will.

## Introduction

So SSM without protection of religious freedoms is now a reality

So, Parliament has passed the same sex marriage bill and has cast our religious freedoms aside as something they can give, and they can take away at their whim. But our freedoms were not granted to us by a willing Parliament, but it is something purchased by blood and smoke by men and women who said, "The government will not dictate my conscience." These courageous people did this in an environment far more hostile than we presently encounter.

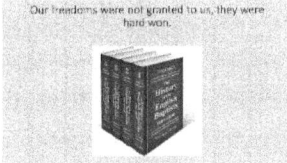

Our freedoms were not granted to us, they were hard won.

I would encourage you to read The *History of the English Baptists* by Thomas Crosby to gain some understanding of how hard won our freedoms were. So, in the face of a nation which, by turning its back on its foundations and so doing, losing its soul as some would argue, it might be helpful to look at a church operating in an earlier hostile world.

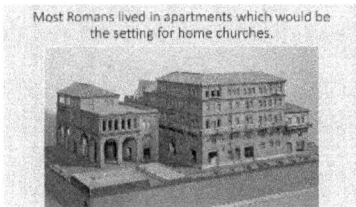

Most Romans lived in apartments which would be the setting for home churches.

Romans was written to home churches with a ragtag congregation where Christianity was considered an aberration. Tacitus, a Roman historian described them as "A race of men hated for their evil practices" and would soon after Paul's letter be violently suppressed. I have heard how the Good Lord provided this chapel which is magnificent for a country church and we thank him for it. But if push comes to shove, and our freedoms are continually eroded, and churches and church schools are faced with the ultimatum, toe the government line or be exposed to financial penalties, what do we do? Deny our faith to protect our assets as the Royal Commission into child abuse is finding that too many have done. They deserve to lose them. But I am talking about conscience, not expediency. Is this building our Christianity? Of course not. It serves us and helps us in our mission. But just like those early churches gathered in the larger homes we could gather together equally well and worship in Barry's shed.

## A look at Romans 12.

What does the 12th chapter of Romans that Betty read mean? It was written to Christians meeting in house churches in Rome, 2000 years ago and the first rule of hermeneutics is that a text means what it meant to the original hearers. To attempt to plumb its depths we need to try and get into the life situation of a long gone time.

Dole queue at Circular Quay in 1930's

Let's be perfectly honest. We would have trouble getting into the mind of my father's generation who had lived through the great depression and two world wars.

Clearing scrub in Kalbar area in the 1890's

How little chance we have of getting into Herman Windolf's[7] generation with the perils of a long sea journey and clearing scrub so thick that no one thought could ever be cleared and that was only the 1860-70. Yet somehow, we have to jump back to a

---

7 The first German Baptist pastor to Queensland and a forefather to many in the congregation. Refer to my book of that title where I edited his reports back to Germany of his travel over in a clipper ship and the start of his ministry at Kalbar.

culture and conditions that are beyond our comprehension here in Tenthill.

Now, of course, the scriptures address matters that are universal, sin and the need of a saviour, holy living, the struggle to do the right thing when often we don't, and the need for certainty and a source of strength in the face of adverse circumstances. For Christians, Romans will never be a book that we can read and pass a judgement over as just being an historical curiosity, rather, until the Lord returns, it will instead, if we let it, judge us, encourage us and strengthen us as needed.

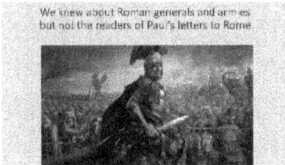

We knew about Roman generals and armies but not the readers of Paul's letters to Rome

But there is still that historical distance and so much of what we knew about Rome was about emperors and generals and armies and conquest and butchery and precious little about the forgotten everyday people of history. These are the people that our Lord set his heart upon and who found eternal hope in circumstances that were, for many if not most, beyond what we would see as tolerable. These are the people Paul wrote to.

Faithful unto death – Pompeii destruction 79 AD

But in 79 AD, Pompeii, a small Roman city on the Bay of Naples was buried under four to six metres of ash, only to be rediscovered after 1500 years and with serious excavation starting about 1750.

Like never before we can see into the lives of the hearers of Pauls book

First it was largely treasure hunting but later serious investigation of the small items of daily life started being recorded and studied.

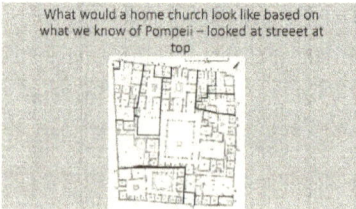

What would a home church look like based on what we know of Pompeii – looked at streeet at top

One block of that city known as the Insula of the Menander has received special attention and if you had a spare $2000 you could purchase a four-volume series that examines it in detail. The archaeology at Pompeii and Herculaneum, another nearby city, has allowed us to grasp some comprehension of the people who first read Paul's letter to the capital of the empire.

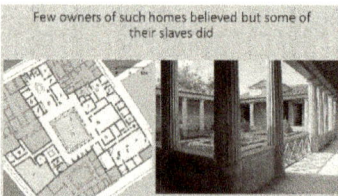

Few owners of such homes believed but some of their slaves did

Based on all this research on this block, one writer put his mind to asking what would a home church be like based on the houses on one street from that block that comprised a baker, craftworkers, a mansion and a bar.

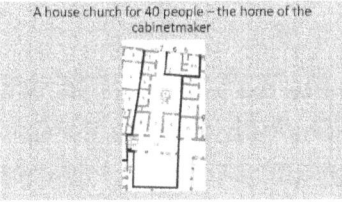

A house church for 40 people – the home of the cabinetmaker

The house of the cabinet maker could host about 30-40 people providing they didn't mind stepping over the tools and work in progress. So with this as a starting point, he suggested a home church would look something like this:

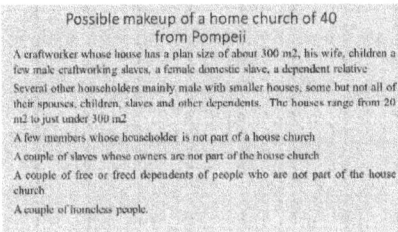

Possible makeup of a home church of 40 from Pompeii

A craftworker whose house has a plan size of about 300 m2, his wife, children a few male craftworking slaves, a female domestic slave, a dependent relative

Several other householders mainly male with smaller houses, some but not all of their spouses, children, slaves and other dependents. The houses range from 20 m2 to just under 300 m2

A few members whose householder is not part of a house church

A couple of slaves whose owners are not part of the house church

A couple of free or freed dependents of people who are not part of the house church

A couple of homeless people.

A craftworker whose house has a plan size of about 300 m2, his wife, children, a few male craftworking slaves, a female domestic slave, a dependent relative

Several other householders mainly male with smaller houses, some but not all of their spouses, children, slaves and other dependents. The houses range from 20 m2 to just under 300 m2

A few members whose householder is not part of a house church

A couple of slaves whose owners are not part of the house church

A couple of free or freed dependents of people who are not part of the house church

A couple of homeless people.

Transposing that to Rome with smaller room sizes you are probably talking 30 people of similar makeup with the addition of a few people renting space in a shared room, just like some of our back packers.

Can you imagine a church more different to the faithful saints that meet at Tenthill? It almost bids the question of how much Romans can ever say to us about living our daily life. Can you get your mind around slavery? For most of these slaves there was only one thing worse than the injustice of living as a chattel and that was freedom, the only freedom most could expect and that was to be thrown on the street when they became sick or too old to work.

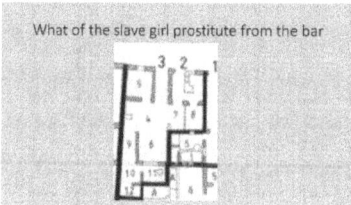
What of the slave girl prostitute from the bar

What about Iris, the slave girl in the bar. We know her name from the graffiti and, that most likely, she had to service the needs of the bar customers for more than food and drink. There were many slaves in the early Christian churches and it was known that female slaves, and not just female slaves, would have been regularly abused. Can you imagine members such as these comprising our congregation? Can you imagine the inner conflict when they heard the words of Paul at the start of our reading "offer your bodies as a living sacrifice, holy and pleasing to God" when there was nothing they could possibly do about living a life that we would call pure? Compare the exclusivity of some branches of present day Christianity with the tolerance and acceptance that must have been required at times back then.

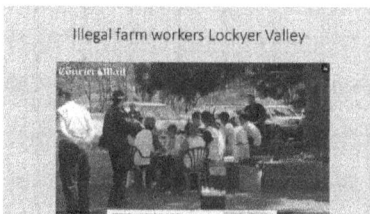
Illegal farm workers Lockyer Valley

Well, here in the Tenthill Valley we don't encounter the open slave markets of present day Libya but, recent media revelations have shown that squalid conditions, defrauded wages and morally unsafe workplaces have and still exist in some places in the agricultural industry in Australia. The word was bandied around last week about contract workers here in the Lockyer. But verse 2 goes on to say, "Do not conform to the pattern of this world, but be transformed by the renewing of your mind. Then you will be able to test and approve what God's will is—his good, pleasing and perfect will." I know that those of us who employ workers, and I have done my fair share also, do so as people of transformed minds, not hiring illegal workers, paying the right wage and providing a safe workplace. With our businesses we always have the battle of cutting costs but never does that include, "let's cheat and abuse our workers." This attitude that comes so naturally might not look very spiritual but make no mistake it is part of our "true and proper worship." I say this to commend you because commendation is due.

The home church members were too ordinary to be seen as loved by God and called to be his holy people

But I also want to challenge you. What of those free or freed men and their families with homes down to 20 m2 when the average house size was about 270 m2? My friend Noe Galzote lived in a 6 metre square building in a slum in Manilla which contained two rooms and a kitchen. When you see that you realise how small 36 m2 is. This was abject poverty but here in Pompeii we had homes down to even 10 m2 and a number at 25 m2 and, of course, no toilet. We are talking about people who are living day to day, barely eking out an existence and whose survival is perilous. The

Romans had their special religious groups who were called out to special closeness to their gods such as the Vestal Virgins. Their exalted status separated them from the plebs and lifted them to a level that ordinary worshippers could not achieve. "The lives of the house church members seemed too ordinary to be special" as they were a ragtag bunch from the lowest sections of society yet Paul speaks to them saying they were loved by God and called to be his holy people (Rom 1:6). How differently our Lord's vision is and how different ours should be of the poor and the common.

To a church with such abject poverty at its very core, Paul said "Share with the Lord's people who are in need. Practise hospitality." I know that some of us, perhaps most of us, have known times of plenty and times of hardship but most of us can't say, "We have experienced such a level of hardship as the early church knew" but hardship by Australian standards does exist around us. We learnt that over ten years ago when Alan Gordon, a previous pastor, did the comparison of our church to our community reflected in the census. We weren't, and we still aren't reaching the poor in our valley or more correctly in the hills. But I have been praying that we will. We could seat another 100 here if we get the seats out of storage. My friends, the call to generosity towards the poor believers was an incredible burden and only the Good Lord keeping his side of the equation by providing ever made it possible.

The outworking of the gospel in our midst is not about staying with the social order that existed 2000 years ago but should be transformational. Loyalty was very much concentrated towards the family, funds were too limited to think very far beyond that. And it wasn't always too crash hot inside the family as, if a newborn baby did not pass the plumbing inspection, it could be exposed on the local garbage heap! If it was fortunate it died. But Paul turns the idea of a self-sufficient family unit on its head, [4]" For just as each of us has one body with many members, and these members do not all have the same function, [5] so in Christ we, though many, form one body, and each member belongs to all the others." As a family business unit our cabinet maker would have known of the interconnectedness of all the members of his household. But also, they knew the hierarchy that existed and also the social distance, the slave was just that. But Paul told them that this interdependence is across households and across social classes and challenged household boundaries. The homeless, the slave, the very poor, in Christ were all interconnected, all as vital as a close family member. You can choose your friends, but you can't choose your family in Christ.

But this flows through to leaders too. The hierarchy in normal society is challenged too. "[6] We have different gifts, according to the grace given to each of us. If your gift is prophesying, then prophesy in accordance with your faith; [7] if it is serving, then serve; if it is teaching, then teach; [8] if it is to encourage, then give encouragement; if it is giving, then give generously; if it is to lead, do it diligently; if it is to show mercy, do it cheerfully." Back then, it would have been easy to have a situation, indeed even for it to be expected for someone to say, you are meeting in my home, I am the biggest giver, so I am appointing the leader and he will be my man, in my pocket so as to speak. We are looking for a new pastor and, as Baptists, the role of appointing this person rests with the congregation. We can't avoid the responsibility to pray and to discern. While education is important, it will not substitute for gifting and character. Back then it might well have been a slave that God had gifted, not the upwardly mobile. Are we prepared to accept leadership from someone from the wrong side of the tracks or with a dubious but forgiven past? But what about the gifts God has given to us. We all have them. Some of these gifts from God require money, to be merciful by generously forgiving or delaying a debt, or cheerfully giving to those in need. Some gifts can be done by the poorest of the poor like giving encouragement or teaching or leading. This is not a matter of the worthy serving out of their bounty to the lesser but of a community sharing what has been gifted them.

My dear dad, may the Good Lord rest his soul, was very highly regarded in the community. In the eyes of most, when I was a young, I was always Edgar Stubbersfield's son. It was much more the case back in the community that received Paul's letter, when honour of the family members was tied up with the status of the head of the household. In our home church, it would only have been the freeborn, only a minority of the members that could have had honour in the society. Again, Paul turns social convention on its head in verse 10, "Be devoted to one another in love. Honour one another above yourselves." But honour in the Roman church is not associated with status. They were all God's children, slave or free. The distinctions our society put up by their society and ours as important, race, gender, or whatever are swept away. We all share god's sonship to the same extent and, in same way, as free born Christians. There is not one of us here that is not worthy of honour and being treated with honour because our father has first honoured them.

## Conclusion

I have come to realise in recent days that my Christianity never was radical enough and at this stage in my life there is probably nothing much that can be done to rectify that. Over the years our society has been turning its back on its maker and the foundation of our culture, the death of a thousand cuts. Now with the new legislation, our society is in for rapid and radical change, change it never expected and change without any safeguards or checks. Increasingly, we are going to have to take a stand based on a conscience made captive to the Word of God. It is going to be a time when, in the history of this church at least, there is the need for radical Christianity as the opponents of the Gospel become increasingly more powerful and active. But the Christ's church has been there before and in some part of the world is going through much worse.

How are we to respond? Paul answers this with the most radical concept of our faith [14] "Bless those who persecute you; bless and do not curse." And "If your enemy is hungry, feed him; if he is thirsty, give him something to drink." There are some things that only the Good Lord can sort out, as he said, "Do not take revenge, my dear friends, but leave room for God's wrath, for it is written: "It is mine to avenge; I will repay,""

So, my friends, let us be radical in our Christianity especially in the way that we love and treat each other and, if the opportunity arises, let us also be radical in our treatment of the enemies of the gospel.

# 7 THE TWO TYPES OF FARMERS

*This communion address is a further attempt to meet Jayson Windolf's request to deliver a communion address which includes a tractor.*

When Jesus stood before Pilate we read in John 18 that he "summoned Jesus and asked him, "Are you the king of the Jews?" [34] "Is that your own idea," Jesus asked, "or did others talk to you about me?" [35] "Am I a Jew?" Pilate replied. "Your own people and chief priests handed you over to me. What is it you have done?" [36] Jesus said, "My kingdom is not of this world. If it were, my servants would fight to prevent my arrest by the Jewish leaders. But now my kingdom is from another place." [37] "You are a king, then!" said Pilate. Jesus answered, "You say that I am a king. In fact, the reason I was born and came into the world is to testify to the truth. Everyone on the side of truth listens to me.""

Two Kinds of Farmers
Those that use red tractors
and those that use green

You all know I am horticulturally challenged. One day Graham Windolf gave me a deep insight. He said, "Ted, there are only two types of farmers, those that use red tractors and those that use green." But I might add a third, those that use real tractors.

And those that use "real" tractors
Driscolls farm 1912

This is my grandfather's traction engine at Driscolls farm in 1912.

You will reasonably ask me, where are all the mod cons? What about GPS? Tick, Generates Plenty of Smoke, What about a cupholder, Tick, he doubled as the fireman, What about a comfortable seat, completely unnecessary, you stood up all day. OK, I grant it was hard work.

Agreed, it was hard dirty work
North St., Gatton

It hasn't been all progress since 1912. This tractor could do things even the Finnish ones can't. You see when he was thirsty Grandfather just threw some leaves in the billy and opened the tap on the boiler and very soon he had a fresh, if somewhat rusty, brew. Hungry, he dusted off the shovel, cracked a couple of eggs onto it along with some bacon and put it in the firebox.

Of course, it is a good thing we have left those days behind, but it hasn't all been progress. Most now have little if any need in an unseen world which they consider probably does not exist anyway. Instead, they have become obsessed with beautiful things, and the latest technology, an easy life and cheap pristine food from a well-stocked supermarket. Even the scientists will eventually ward off death we are promised. The Apostle Paul's words in Romans 14, [17] For the kingdom of God is not a matter of eating and drinking, but of righteousness, peace and joy in the Holy Spirit, are incomprehensible to them.

As Christians we are convinced of the reality and permanence of an unseen world where the toil and troubles of this transient and everchanging world will cease. A kingdom whose access is only through the blood of our crucified saviour and where our true citizenship resides.

# 8 WOE IS ME

*This sermon was a preparation for the commencement of the ministry of our new pastor, Dale Buchanan Pastor Tim was off on paternal leave after the safe delivery of their third child.*

**Reading**: 1 Cor. 9:[13] Don't you know that those who serve in the temple get their food from the temple, and that those who serve at the altar share in what is offered on the altar? [14] In the same way, the Lord has commanded that those who preach the gospel should receive their living from the gospel.

[15] But I have not used any of these rights. And I am not writing this in the hope that you will do such things for me, for I would rather die than allow anyone to deprive me of this boast. [16] For when I preach the gospel, I cannot boast, since I am compelled to preach. Woe to me if I do not preach the gospel! [17] If I preach voluntarily, I have a reward; if not voluntarily, I am simply discharging the trust committed to me. [18] What then is my reward? Just this: that in preaching the gospel I may offer it free of charge, and so not make full use of my rights as a preacher of the gospel.

**Text:** 2 Tim. 4 [1] In the presence of God and of Christ Jesus, who will judge the living and the dead, and in view of his appearing and his kingdom, I give you this charge: [2] preach the word; be prepared in season and out of season; correct, rebuke and encourage – with great patience and careful instruction. [3] For the time will come when people will not put up with sound doctrine. Instead, to suit their own desires, they will gather round them a great number of teachers to say what their itching ears want to hear. [4] They will turn their ears away from the truth and turn aside to myths. [5] But you, keep your head in all situations, endure hardship, do the work of an evangelist, discharge all the duties of your ministry.

When Pastor Tim asked me to preach on what was initially planned as next Sunday, I asked if he had a text or a subject. He pointed out that with Pastor Dale starting next week that that might be a dead giveaway. Considering that, I have chosen a text about a changing of the guard, the word of a dying man to his heir apparent and a passing of the baton seems appropriate. But before I get started, what do you think of our new pulpit? Fourteen men applied to stand behind this pulpit and preach the word as Pastor of Tenthill Baptist Church. Perhaps it is a sign that things are stirring, and we will be again preaching the word "in season". We must thank the search committee for a job well done in their recommendation. And of course, Pastor Ian for ten years of service. This pulpit was made with love and skill by our brother, Selwyn. He used a high grade of silky oak, one of our finest cabinet timbers and the top is big enough to carry this big Bible and my notes easily. I think it is good enough to grace any Baptist church and I can say without a doubt, it is the second best pulpit I have ever stood behind.

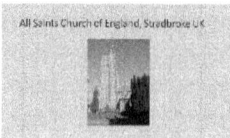
All Saints Church of England, Stradbroke UK

Yes, I have seen one better. Years ago, I was driving through Stradbroke in Suffolk, in the United Kingdom with my friend Pastor Steere and he took me inside for a look at All Saints Church of England.

JC Ryle, Priest at the church 1861-1872

Back in 1870, its minister, a leading evangelical at the time, J C Ryle started a fund to renovate the church. As a pastor and later bishop, he was convinced that Christianity stands or falls depending on its relation to the word of God and to the Holy Spirit.

He wrote many books, including *Holiness*, one I read when I was young and need to read again and take to heart.

The best wooden pulpit I have stood behind

As I stood in his old timber pulpit I saw how he had carved into the top, "Woe is me if I preach not the Gospel." Selwyn, how I wish wood carving was one of your many woodworking skills because I would ask you to carve those very same words deep in our own pulpit.

Oh, you have never seen this old Bible of mine. As I said, it's a big one. It has a soft chamois leather cover, wide margin, rice paper and is a New Scofield Reference Bible. I didn't get it because it was of a somewhat dubious reference system, but it was recommended to us by an old lecturer in Bible college for open air work. See how it drapes over my hand. You can use it in the open and the wind won't catch the pages. You don't need a pulpit to preach the word and while it might be good to have that text carved into a piece of wood, it means little if the words, "Woe is me if I preach not the gospel", are not carved deep into the heart of anyone who stands in front of you. And this, in a roundabout way, brings us to our text., "In the presence of God and of Christ Jesus, who will judge the living and the dead, and in view of his appearing and his kingdom, I give you this charge: preach the word".

We have, in the passage I read, the contrast of substance to illusion. We all know Hebrews 11:1 well. "Now faith is the substance of things hoped for, the evidence of things not seen." Critics of our faith would say it is all "pie in the sky" and that we are deceiving ourselves and, if they are right, we are of all people to be pitied. Yet we believe in an unseen world and an unseen future that we hold, not as more real than this present existence, but of more value and permanence.

From the Apostles Creed

On the third day he rose again;
he ascended into heaven,
he is seated at the right hand of the Father,
and he will come to judge the living and the dead.

There is a judge of the living and the dead, of this the early church had no doubt of this. You find the same expression in Acts 10:2 and 1 Pet. 4:5, as well as in the writings of early church fathers and the Apostles Creed. Into that sad and sorry world came a reality that gave hope to the poorest and the most oppressed. The gospel assured them that God saw, that he cared and that there would be a time when every tear would be wiped away. That the cry, "How long Oh Lord," would one day be answered. This for them was not an illusion but the substance for all that endured to the end.

Neither should we be in any doubt that Jesus who came once to save will come again to complete our salvation but also to judge. Paul gave Timothy the charge to preach the word because, not only the false teachers will have to give an account, but also Timothy himself and all those that he ministered to and looked to him as a shepherd. The same theme of the day of judgement is taken up again in verse 6: "For I am already being poured out like a drink offering, and the time for my departure is near. [7] I have fought the good fight, I have finished the race, I have kept the faith. [8] Now there is in store for me the crown of righteousness, which the Lord, the righteous Judge, will award to me on that day—and not only to me, but also to all who have longed for his appearing." And Paul thinks of that day when he will stand before his saviour and strive no more. But in that Already-Not yet dichotomy which is our Christian faith Paul already stood before his saviour. This, my friends, is the substance of our faith.

Well might Paul say, in the presence of God and Christ Jesus because there was no one else, except probably a Roman soldier guarding him. Paul wrote to Timothy in verse 16 "At my first defence, no one came to my support, but everyone deserted me. May it not be held against them" and here "Do your best to come to me quickly, [10] for Demas, because he loved this world, has deserted me and has gone to Thessalonica. Crescens has gone to Galatia, and Titus to Dalmatia. [11] Only Luke is with me. Get Mark and bring him with you, because he is helpful to me in my ministry. [12] I sent Tychicus to Ephesus. [13] When you come, bring the cloak that I left with Carpus at Troas, and my scrolls, especially the parchments. And that, in a roundabout way, brings us to what might have been our text, "When you come, bring the cloak that I left with Carpus at Troas"

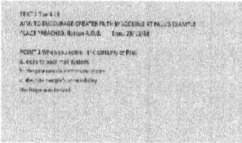

When I was preparing lectures on Hermeneutics a long time ago I included a sermon on just that text. Here is the outline:

TEXT 2 Tim 4:13

AIM: TO ENCOURAGE GREATER FAITH BY LOOKING AT PAUL'S EXAMPLE

PLACE PREACHED: Gatton A.O.G.      Date: 25/12/88

POINT 1 When you come - the certainty of Paul

a. despite poor mail system
b. despite unsafe communications
c. despite people's unreliability.
His hope was In God.

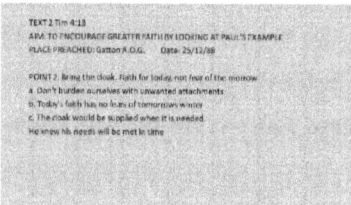

POINT 2. Bring the cloak. Faith for today, not fear of the morrow

a. Don't burden ourselves with unwanted attachments
b. Today's faith has no fears of tomorrows winter
c. The cloak would be supplied when it is needed.
He knew his needs will be met in time

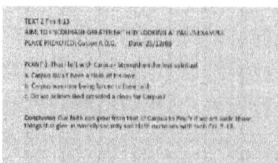

POINT 3. That I left with Carpus - Strengthen the less spiritual

a. Carpus didn't have a cloak of his own
b. Carpus was now being forced to have faith
c. Do we believe God provided a cloak for Carpus?

**Conclusion**-Our faith can grow from that of Carpus to Paul's if we set aside those things that give us worldly security and cloth ourselves with faith Col. 3:12.

A minister was reading my lectures one day and he praised my skill in preparing such a wonderful sermon, pity he didn't understand what went before where I was saying that you can make any text say exactly what you want it to say. It is utter claptrap and an illusion of spiritual depth.

The charge to Timothy to preach the word is also a charge to all laymen and women who have committed themselves to the substance of an unseen world. All of us are called to speak the word at the very least in our conduct in an age "when people will not put up with sound doctrine. Instead, to suit their own desires, they will gather round them a great number of teachers to say what their itching ears want to hear." Paul describes an age where claptrap and illusion satisfies because it does not challenge anyone to stand alone and live a holy and redeemed life. It doesn't challenge anyone to dare to live standing in the presence of an unseen God. The gathered multitude with ears itching for anything but the truth stands in stark contrast to the lonely shackled Paul. The responsibility that comes with standing behind this pulpit is enormous, yes, but make no mistake, by sitting in the pew does not absolve us of the challenge to love sound doctrine, to speak with our actions as well as our mouth and, if necessary, to stand alone.

I noted that a latest biography of J C Ryle was entitled *Prepared to Stand Alone*.

Being prepared, in season and out of season - the commentators have different opinions, do you preach the word whether you are running on full or empty or continue to preach the word whether people are listening and responding or not? Consider the former option, an illusion we can face is that of a God who was never satisfied with our efforts. Well, we have all had to go to work when we didn't feel like it, but you can't run on empty forever. Paul surely was not telling Timothy to work unrelentingly until he had a burnout, something of which we all run the risk. We had a look at the need for a balanced life from Martin Luther a couple of months back. He preached the word, yes but he also slept, and he drank Whittenburg beer with his friends and let the word do its work. Maybe in this valley he might have preached, slept and drank flat whites at Sorellas with his friends. There are some very perceptive words I heard some years ago, "When the Lord finds a willing horse, the Devil will flog him to death."

On balance, the command was more likely aimed at preaching and for that matter, being about all our Christian endeavours whether there is a good response or virtually none. This church has been blessed to know the good times, but it is no different to other churches in that it has known disappointment in its presenting and representing the good news to a community that loves the illusions of this world to the certainty of Christ's kingdom. Well, we might say, no-one is listening, so we will shake the dust of them from our feet and stay in an insulated holy huddle inside the safety of these walls. If Jesus wants to save their souls he can drag them across the threshold of this building. We will just stay here until Jesus returns and takes us safely home. God forbid, it is the very fact of our Lord's return, when he will judge the living and the dead, that causes Paul to give the charge, "Preach the word."

My friends, pastors can know the disappointment that can come from preaching to an unresponsive world but this text tells us to look closer to home. There is no promise of an eager response even on the part of God's people. In other places in his letters to Timothy, Paul puts the emphasis on people being deceived (1 Tim. 4:1-2, 5:15, 6:5, 2 Tim. 3:6-7, 13) here he lays the blame at the feet of straying believers. They won't put up with sound doctrine. They will gather around them. They have itching ears. They will turn aside to myths. They will turn from substance to illusion.

Timothy, don't just be a pastor correcting, rebuking, encouraging but be an evangelist as well. From Paul's letters to Timothy we see that he had a natural timidity. For example, I remind you to fan into flame the gift that is within you (2 Tim 1;6). I can imagine him thinking, "But what is the point of speaking the truth when men and women want to turn their ears away and listen to people who will give them an illusory god, or the greatest of illusions, no god if that is their choice, in exactly the image they want to see." I never became a street preacher and I never became an evangelist. It is a gift that the Good Lord did not give me, but I am blessed to know some and have been honoured to partner with them. I have seen the changes when a man or a woman stops chasing illusions and comes and stands in the certainty of a loving friend whose burden is easy. If this church ever loses its love for sinners and the desire to share God's love with them then "Woe is us."

That brings us back again to the pulpit in Stradbroke All Saints Church. As you stand in the pulpit you can see texts written on the cross beams of the roof.

Facing the congregation:

God be merciful to me a sinner,
I will arise and go to my father,
Create in me a clean heart O God,
Search the scriptures prove all things,
Believe in the Lord Jesus Christ and thou shalt be saved.

It starts off, "God be merciful to me a sinner," then, "I will arise and go to my father," then, "Create in me a clean heart O God," then, "Search the scriptures prove all things," and finally, "Believe in the Lord Jesus Christ and thou shalt be saved." If our minister has not tasted of the mercy and grace of the judge of the living and the dead, if we have not tasted of that same grace and know the certainty of it, then woe is us for what word do we have to preach and what word can our lives express? It certainly won't be, "be reconciled to God."

Facing the priest:

Strive to enter in at the strait gate.
We have redemption through his blood,
We have an advocate with the father.

From where the congregation sat they saw different verses and they described what should be the response of all who hear the word of grace preached from Selwyn's pulpit as well. Strive to enter in at the straight gate. We have redemption through his blood. We have an advocate with the father. For those who hear the word, the command is to move from the illusions that have satisfied to the substance of reconciliation with the judge of the living and the dead.

I should have had a stronger conclusion I know, and maybe I could have taken a line out of my hermeneutics lectures – "point weak here, thump the pulpit." This pulpit isn't really made to thump but it is made to preach from. May the gospel of reconciliation go out from it clearly and may the word that is preached find willing hearers.

# 9 TRULY, TRULY I SAY UNTO YOU

*The Gatton Baptists were on Church camp for the weekend so I was asked to preach to the "stragglers". Pastor Doug was going through the Verily, verily sayings of Jesus and it fell to me to deal with the statements in Chapter 5.*

**Reading:** The healing at the pool, John 5:1-15

John 5 Some time later, Jesus went up to Jerusalem for one of the Jewish festivals. [2] Now there is in Jerusalem near the Sheep Gate a pool, which in Aramaic is called Bethesda and which is surrounded by five covered colonnades. [3] Here a great number of disabled people used to lie – the blind, the lame, the paralysed. [5] One who was there had been an invalid for thirty-eight years. [6] When Jesus saw him lying there and learned that he had been in this condition for a long time, he asked him, 'Do you want to get well?'

[7] 'Sir,' the invalid replied, 'I have no-one to help me into the pool when the water is stirred. While I am trying to get in, someone else goes down ahead of me.'

[8] Then Jesus said to him, 'Get up! Pick up your mat and walk.' [9] At once the man was cured; he picked up his mat and walked.

The day on which this took place was a Sabbath, [10] and so the Jewish leaders said to the man who had been healed, 'It is the Sabbath; the law forbids you to carry your mat.'

[11] But he replied, 'The man who made me well said to me, "Pick up your mat and walk."'

[12] So they asked him, 'Who is this fellow who told you to pick it up and walk?'

[13] The man who was healed had no idea who it was, for Jesus had

slipped away into the crowd that was there.

[14] Later Jesus found him at the temple and said to him, 'See, you are well again. Stop sinning or something worse may happen to you.' [15] The man went away and told the Jewish leaders that it was Jesus who had made him well.

**Text:** John 5 [16] So, because Jesus was doing these things on the Sabbath, the Jewish leaders began to persecute him. [17] In his defence Jesus said to them, 'My Father is always at his work to this very day, and I too am working.' [18] For this reason they tried all the more to kill him; not only was he breaking the Sabbath, but he was even calling God his own Father, making himself equal with God.

[19] Jesus gave them this answer: 'Very truly I tell you, the Son can do nothing by himself; he can do only what he sees his Father doing, because whatever the Father does the Son also does. [20] For the Father loves the Son and shows him all he does. Yes, and he will show him even greater works than these, so that you will be amazed. [21] For just as the Father raises the dead and gives them life, even so the Son gives life to whom he is pleased to give it. [22] Moreover, the Father judges no one, but has entrusted all judgment to the Son, [23] that all may honour the Son just as they honour the Father. Whoever does not honour the Son does not honour the Father who sent him.

[24] 'Very truly I tell you, whoever hears my word and believes him who sent me has eternal life and will not be judged but has crossed over from death to life. [25] Very truly I tell you, a time is coming and has now come when the dead will hear the voice of the Son of God and those who hear will live. [26] For as the Father has life in himself, so he has granted the Son also to have life in himself.

<sup>27</sup> And he has given him authority to judge because he is the Son of Man.

<sup>28</sup> 'Do not be amazed at this, for a time is coming when all who are in their graves will hear his voice <sup>29</sup> and come out – those who have done what is good will rise to live, and those who have done what is evil will rise to be condemned. <sup>30</sup> By myself I can do nothing; I judge only as I hear, and my judgment is just, for I seek not to please myself but him who sent me.

You know, I have reached that stage in my life when, if I am talking to other people my own age, I find I have to repeat myself a lot. It comes with the territory, I am afraid. Fortunately, it's not because my short-term memory is failing, not yet at least, but because of hardness of hearing by the other oldies. Jesus was a lot younger than me and in his prime but here we find him repeating himself in verses 26-30 what he just said in the preceding seven verses, when he says he will raise the dead and he will be the judge of all men.

This passage may contain repetition and lack the striking expressions such as "the bread of life" and the "I am" sayings but it is crucial to our understanding our faith. "Nowhere else in the gospels do we find our Lord making such a formal, systematic, orderly, regular statement of his own unity with the Father, His divine commission and authority, and the proofs of His Messiahship, as we find"[8] here. It is not surprising then that we find "Truly, truly" three times in our passage because as the old Anglican divine, J C Ryle described this passage as, "One of the deepest things in the Bible."[9]

---

8 Morris, Leon. *The Gospel of John*. 311 (Quoting JC Ryle)
9 Morris. *John ...*, 311.

But before we look at that, first we need to look at our context. Jesus came to the Pool of Bethsaida and gave a worthwhile life back to a man that has been an invalid for 38 years. How long he has been there, who knows, but long enough to have virtually given up on the miraculous healing. How long do you sit around before you figure that a healing pool is load of old codswallop? His answer to Jesus is not that it is bogus but that he can't get in the pool fast enough. I wonder what he saw that caused him to stay? We are not sure what was happening at this healing pool built outside of the walls of Jerusalem. What the commentators seem to agree on that it wasn't quite kosher and he wasn't told to wash there. In the 1st century BC, natural caves to the east of the two pools of Bethsaida were turned into small baths, as part of an Asklepion, where the pagans went for healing. But whatever was happening, this man was perfectly happy to break the strict interpretation of the Law by actively trying to get healed on the sabbath.

Now, what would you say if I announced this morning, "In an attempt to raise the spirituality of this church, I have arranged for Dr. Rosenberg to come along after the service and circumcise all the men. I have been studying the scriptures and I have learnt that we need to be good Jews before we even attempt to become good Christians?' I hope what you would not say is "Who's first," but "Where have you been these last 2000 years? That old chestnut was sorted out during the time of the apostles." Now, you have a similar thing with the Sabbath. John's gospel was written after Paul's battles with Judaisers that we read of in Acts. He wrote to a church that no longer needed to be freed from the Sabbath laws and traditions.[10] Yet the Sabbath, central to Jewish practice, is critical to understanding the purpose of the signs of the paralytic and also the man born blind a few chapters later.

And it is "Signs". John does not have miracles. He has "signs" and only seven of them. When he wrote his gospel, he ignored much of what he knew and focused on seven signs that showed who Jesus was. His signs are more striking than the miracles in Matthew, Mark and Luke. Jairus's daughter was dead a short while compared to Lazarus dead four days and decaying, healing the blind compared to healing the man born blind, and healing the woman who had been bleeding for twelve years and here a man who was an invalid for 38 years. These were signs done in the open and no mention about keeping quiet about them. They were meant to make you stop in your tracks and make a judgment about who was standing before you. Jesus to this day demands that you pass judgement on who he is.

10Barratt, *Gospel…*,77

| REFERENCE | EVENT | JESUS, THE MASTER OF |
|---|---|---|
| 2:1-11 | water into wine | Quality - made a change that normally takes months |
| 4:46-54 | healing nobleman's son | Distance - boy was 20 miles away |
| 5:1-9 | Healing of the impotent man | Time - afflicted for 38 years |
| 6:1-14 | Feeding the five thousand | quantity |
| 6:16-21 | Walking on water | natural law |
| 9:1-12 | Healing of the man born blind | misfortune |
| 11:1-46 | The raising of Lazarus | death |

Jesus healed two protracted disabilities on the Sabbath, here and in John 9, with the man born blind and both of those to avoid conflict with the Jews, could have easily waited another day.[11] After all, the man had been an invalid for 38 years. Another day would not make any difference to him in the overall scheme of his life. There was no way he was going to get into the water between now and then! Jesus further complicated matters by commanding the invalided man to break the Sabbath (5:8), something, as I

11Pidcock-Lester. Karen. "John 5:1-9." *Interpretation*, (January 2007) 61

mentioned, he was quite prepared to do already. Carrying an empty bed on the Sabbath was forbidden.[12] The teachers of the Law had worked out what was permissible on the sabbath and one of their rules forbade carrying an object between a private domain and the public domain, or for a distance of 4 cubits (1.8 metres) within the public domain.[13] And later in the healing of the man born blind, kneading clay to apply to the blind eyes was also forbidden.[14]

In all the gospels, Jesus seemed to provoke dispute on the Sabbath but, in John, the arguments to heal on that day are not based on humanitarian grounds (Luke 13:15, 14:5) but on theology. You find theological reasons also in Matthew where the priests work on the sabbath and now something greater than the temple is present (Matt 12:5-6). But in John, it is a different theological reason, and it revolves around God's relationship to the creation and the Sabbath rest. Seeing miracles that are creation like, the Jews, and in John's gospel, the word "Jews" has a special meaning, who were controlled by their oral tradition, respond with spiritual paralysis, forgetting that the Sabbath was once linked to the vitality of creation.[15] Rather than show proper Sabbath conduct, these signs "establish the blindness of the 'Jewish' judgement of the Son".[16]

In Exodus 20:11, in the ten commandments, God said, "For in six days the Lord made the heavens and the earth, the sea and all that is in them, but he rested on the seventh day. Therefore, the Lord blessed the Sabbath day and made it holy." What a thorny problem it raised. We know Genesis 2 "By the sixth day God had

---

12Mishna *Sabbath* 10:5, 7:2

13Mishna *Sabbath* 7:2

14Mishna *Sabbath* 7:2

15Brodie, Gospel..., 240

16Weiss, Herold, The Sabbath in the Fourth Gospel. *Journal of Biblical Literature* 110, 317

finished the work he had been doing. So on the seventh day he rested from all his work.[3] Then God blessed the seventh day and made it holy, because on it he rested from all the work of creating that he had done."  Hang on Ted, in Genesis, wasn't that the seventh day, not the sixth that he finished?  The Greek translations the apostles used, the Septuagint, and a heap of other early transitions say "sixth day".  How can you have the almighty ceasing on the seventh day and breaking the Sabbath when we Jews stopped on the sixth.  Let's give the Almighty some help and fix the mistake he made when he gave us Genesis.

Healing on the Sabbath was a real thorny issue.  Progressive Pharisees could only allow Sabbath prayer for the sick[17] while others would allow only sufficient care to be done so as to stabilise any wound or illness but do nothing to alleviate it.  The Jews understood God's creative works were finished when he entered his Sabbath,[18] so we have a God who was supposed to be resting. But people became sick on the Sabbath and they also recovered. In the same way, people were born and people died and went to their judgement on the sabbath and yet the giving and taking of life and of judgment was only God's prerogative.  Some also realised that God continued his creative acts but working on the sabbath was his prerogative, and his alone.  Murderous hatred was raised among the Jews (5:18) who understood the implication that Sabbath healings declare the nature of the former carpenter from Nazareth and now itinerant preacher and miracle worker as God's Son and his equal.

The Father working "until now" (5:17) highlights the saving activity of the father in the work of the Son"[19].  Jesus was not destroying the Sabbath but releasing it "from the weekly

---

17Keener, *Gospel…*, 785-6

[18]Beasley-Murray, George R., *John*. (Waco: Word Books, 1987), 74.
19Wiss, *Sabbath…*, 317

chronological cycle". Life in its totality was lived in an eschatological Sabbath as one theologian described it.[20] For us, we would say that now all worship is done in Spirit and truth, there is now no correct place to worship (4:21-23) nor a correct day.

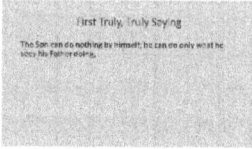

First Truly, Truly Saying

The Son can do nothing by himself; he can do only what he sees his Father doing,

In our first very truly saying, Jesus only does what his Father does (5:19) but more, he can only do what his father does. Based on the Biblical examples, including Adam (Gen 3:5), Nebuchadnezzar (Dan 4:29), and Pharaoh (Ex 5:2), the Jews thought equality with God was independence from him.[21] For Jesus, equality meant utter dependence. John records the very clear statement of Jesus that he and his father are one (10:30) but he did not have in mind a mirror image for "then the reality would belong entirely with the Father".[22] The relationship is better pictured by a skilled tradesman teaching his son,[23] just as Joseph taught Jesus his carpentry trade by seeing and showing (5:19-20). Jesus was doing the work only he had, not just the right and power and to do, but also the skill and training.[24]

The first work of the father's that was entrusted to the son was to give life, "For just as the Father raises the dead and gives them life, even so the Son gives life to whom he is pleased to give it." The command to the invalid healed at the pool was to stop sinning. To those in the world of spiritual death which is the consequence of sin, he has the power to grant life. The only threat to that life is further sin. The second work is to judge, "Moreover, the Father judges no one, but has entrusted all judgment to the Son." But

---

20 Wiss, *Sabbath...*, 319

21 Barrett, *Gospel...*, 256, Philo Allegorical Interpretation 1,49

22 Haenchen, *John 1 ...*, 250

23 Haenchen, *John 1 ...*, 250

24 Beasley-Murray *John...*, 75

here, don't think of the big stick. The corollary to giving life is vindicating the good

Vindicate me, O God,
And plead my cause against an ungodly nation;
Oh, deliver me from the deceitful and unjust man! Psm 43:1

For the LORD will judge His people
And have compassion on His servants,
When He sees that *their* power is gone,
And *there is* no one *remaining,* bond or free Dt 32:36

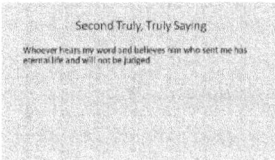

Second Truly, Truly Saying

Whoever hears my word and believes him who sent me has eternal life and will not be judged

Those that stood before Jesus here in Chapter 5 and heard his words had the opportunity to receive life and God's vindication. That is the second Truly, truly in our passage, "Whoever hears my word and believes him who sent me has eternal life and will not be judged but has crossed over from death to life".

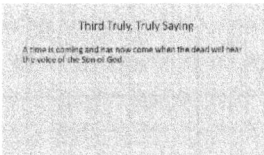

Third Truly, Truly Saying

A time is coming and has now come when the dead will hear the voice of the Son of God.

But there is a third saying. "I tell you, a time is coming and has now come when the dead will hear the voice of the Son of God and those who hear will live." I spoke at the beginning about Jesus repeating himself, what of it. First, consider this table

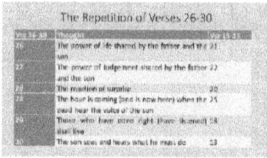

The Repetition of Verses 26-30

| Vs 36-30 | Thought | Vss 19-25 |
|---|---|---|
| 26 | The power of life shared by the father and the son | 21 |
| 27 | The power of Judgement shared by the father and the son | 22 |
| 28 | The reaction of surprise | 20 |
| 28 | The hour is coming (and is now here) when the dead hear the voice of the son | 25 |
| 29 | Those who have done right (have listened) shall live | 19 |
| 30 | The son sees and hears what he must do | 19 |

While the words and thoughts are very similar, the theology is very different and the imagery swings from the spiritually dead who gain life by hearing the Father's son and moves to the son of man, from the vision of Daniel (7:13) and the final judgment. It is not the repetition of old age and forgetfulness. In verses 36-30 we have moved from those who are spiritually dead to those who are in their grave.

Can These Bones Live?

Again, it echoes Daniel with his vision of the resurrection of the dead, some to eternal life and others to eternal shame. The dead also will be given life at the hearing of his voice. It is a claim as staggering as the vision of the valley of dry bones. " "Dry bones, hear the word of the LORD! 5 This is what the Sovereign LORD says to these bones: "I will make breath enter you, and you will come to life".

The two passages give the dichotomy which is a characteristic of John. Again, to use the terms of the theologians, *Realised eschatology* and *Final eschatology*, or the much simpler *already but not yet*. There is the present opportunity to receive life and it is offered here and it is received here, yet death still intervenes but it can't destroy that life. That hour to hear and believe is coming, yes, but is also now here. Twice Jesus urges his hearers to respond, Truly, truly, why would you stand back in disbelief when eternal life is offered freely, where his favourable judgment is already passed on you. But there is something equally certain. Truly, truly, there is a future eternal life beyond the one we now know. It can be a life of honour or one of shame and we will all hear that call. I urge you, choose life.

.

# 10 GRACE AND PEACE IN ABUNDANCE

*In November 2018, Pastor Dale Buchanan and his family came to Tenthill with Dale taking up the senior pastor's role. His first preaching series was on 1 Peter and I was given the task of giving the following sermon as he preached through the book.*

**Reading and Text:** 1 Peter 3:8-22

[8] Finally, all of you, be like-minded, be sympathetic, love one another, be compassionate and humble. [9] Do not repay evil with evil or insult with insult. On the contrary, repay evil with blessing, because to this you were called so that you may inherit a blessing. [10] For,

'Whoever would love life
   and see good days
must keep their tongue from evil
   and their lips from deceitful speech.
[11] They must turn from evil and do good;
   they must seek peace and pursue it.
[12] For the eyes of the Lord are on the righteous
   and his ears are attentive to their prayer,
but the face of the Lord is against those who do evil.'

[13] Who is going to harm you if you are eager to do good? [14] But even if you should suffer for what is right, you are blessed. 'Do not fear their threats; do not be frightened.' [15] But in your hearts revere Christ as Lord. Always be prepared to give an answer to everyone who asks you to give the reason for the hope that you have. But do this with gentleness and respect, [16] keeping a clear conscience, so that those who speak maliciously against your good behaviour in Christ may be ashamed of their slander. [17] For it is better, if it is God's will, to suffer for doing good than for doing evil. [18] For Christ also suffered once for sins, the righteous for the unrighteous,

to bring you to God. He was put to death in the body but made alive in the Spirit. [19] After being made alive, he went and made proclamation to the imprisoned spirits – [20] to those who were disobedient long ago when God waited patiently in the days of Noah while the ark was being built. In it only a few people, eight in all, were saved through water, [21] and this water symbolises baptism that now saves you also – not the removal of dirt from the body but the pledge of a clear conscience towards God. It saves you by the resurrection of Jesus Christ, [22] who has gone into heaven and is at God's right hand – with angels, authorities and powers in submission to him."

## Introduction

For most people living at the time when Peter wrote his letter, life was, as one historian described it, "solitary, poor, nasty, brutish and short." For the Christians, a shadow was being cast over a life that already none of us would have chosen to live. Yet, knowing this, Peter opens this letter to Paul's churches with the greeting and hope "Grace and peace be yours in abundance."

Nero

The setting to this epistle is something like this: Peter and Paul are together in Rome during the European spring of 64. Paul goes off to Spain leaving behind his helpers Mark and Sylvanus who are mentioned in Peter's letter. In July, Rome burns and three months later Nero, in an attempt to shift the blame away from himself, accuses the Christians of lighting the fire. The Roman government, that had previously been fair in its dealing with Christians, changed virtually overnight and all hell broke loose upon the saints. Peter most likely died at this time.

The Recipients of 1 Peter

It was a change that would extend to the far borders of the empire, even to the recipients of this letter in the provinces of Pontus, Galatia, Cappadocia, Asia and Bithynia. Tacitus, a Roman historian, said of this time:

"a vast multitude were convicted, not so much for the crime of burning the city, but for hatred of the human race. And perishing they were additionally made into sports: they were killed by dogs by having the hides of beasts attached to them, or they were nailed to crosses or set aflame, and, when the daylight passed away, they were used as night-time lamps. Nero gave his own gardens for this spectacle."

Grace and peace be yours in abundance.

**Point 1. A life well lived**

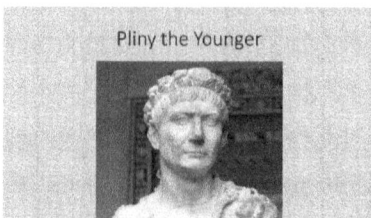

Pliny the Younger

A little less than sixty years later, Pliny the Younger, governor of

Bithinia and Pontus, the area where our letter was sent, wrote to the Emperor Trajan asking his advice on how to deal with Christians. He was a lawyer but inexperienced in trying Christians. What was happening was that he would get anonymous tipoffs that someone was a Christian. He would torture then try them and give them three opportunities to curse Christ and offer sacrifice to the Roman gods and the Emperor. If they refused, he killed them. He had been told that a true Christian would never deny and curse Jesus. Trajan wrote back saying to just keep going the way you are except don't investigate anonymous complaints.

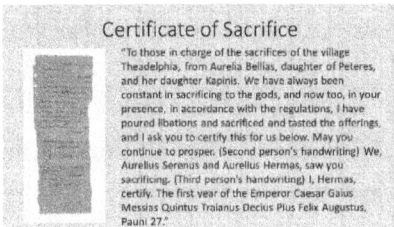

Certificate of Sacrifice

"To those in charge of the sacrifices of the village Theadelphia, from Aurelia Bellias, daughter of Peteres, and her daughter Kapinis. We have always been constant in sacrificing to the gods, and now too, in your presence, in accordance with the regulations, I have poured libations and sacrificed and tasted the offerings, and I ask you to certify this for us below. May you continue to prosper. (Second person's handwriting) We, Aurelius Serenus and Aurelius Hermas, saw you sacrificing. (Third person's handwriting) I, Hermas, certify. The first year of the Emperor Caesar Gaius Messias Quintus Traianus Decius Pius Felix Augustus, Pauni 27."

This is all in the lifespan and quite possibly the experience of some who heard the original letter being read in the congregation. But not only did they hear this letter, they held on to it recognizing something of universal application for every church in every age. If they hadn't, we wouldn't have it now. Evil and insult were to be the lot of many in these provinces in Asia Minor and also the world over ever since. What does Peter say, "Take up your sword and follow me", "Give as good as you get?" "But when they arrest you, do not worry about what to say or how to say it. At that time you will be given an even better insult." No, it was grace and peace be yours in abundance.

For Peter, on the night Jesus was betrayed, there wasn't enough evidence to convict. Two of the three times he denied the Lord were before a servant girl. How Pliny the Younger found "out what the truth [about Christianity] was by torturing two female slaves who were called deaconesses." We can probably assume that they, like others, refused the three opportunities to curse Jesus and live. What were the vile practices worthy of death that he learned from these poor slave girls? "That they were accustomed to meet on a fixed day before dawn and sing responsively a hymn to Christ as to a god, and to bind themselves by oath (the word is sacrament, the one we use of baptism and communion), not to some crime, but not to commit fraud, theft, or adultery, not falsify their trust, nor to refuse to return a trust when called upon to do so.

Despite people who acted this way being considered worthy only of death, this is exactly the kind of life Peter called them to, a life that is above reproach. He urged them to live a life that seeks and pursues after grace and peace. But this is not the peace that the Desert Fathers sought. Martyrdom was the lot of many in the provinces this letter was sent to, but eventually the emperor was converted. Christianity was legalised and martyrdom for the Christian faith, at least in the Roman empire, ceased. What do you do when you long to die the martyr's death and a martyrs crown and that is taken from you? In Egypt initially, individuals went out into the desert and the "solitude, austerity, and sacrifice of the desert was seen ... as an alternative to martyrdom, which was formerly seen by many Christians as the highest form of sacrifice." Just alone with Jesus and the desert wind thinking wonderful thoughts about their Lord and Saviour.

But the Christian life is not meant to be solitary. It is meant to be lived in the full view and in the midst and judgement of others. Yes, in the desert Jesus can see you because his eyes are on the righteous but the sacrifice that Peter envisaged was a life that was lived so well that it gave no reasonable cause for anyone to speak ill of them or of Christ. Tragically, we have seen that the lives of many of our church leaders have been treasonous and have given not just the enemies of the cross but also many innocents that should have sheltered under it, reasonable cause to speak ill of our Lord and our faith. They did not keep their tongue from evil nor their lips from deceitful speech and they did not turn from evil and do good. They will die unwept, unmourned and unsung.

## Point 2. The response to a life well lived

From Verse 13

"The real purpose of Peter has now been reached, namely, to enlighten, comfort, and strengthen. The readers in suffering and trial. They have had some taste of it in their previous experience; now there is the prospect that these sufferings will become far more severe"

From verse 13, as one commentator said, "The real purpose of Peter has now been reached, namely to enlighten, comfort, and strengthen. The readers in suffering and trial. They have had some taste of it in their previous experience; now there is the prospect that these sufferings will become far more severe" "Who is going to harm you if you are eager to do good?" Well the two deaconesses could start by giving you a long list. And all of this suffering was in the name of justice. it is not surprising that the key word and concept in 1 Peter is "suffering for Christ." Some form of the word "suffer" occurs some sixteen times in the book. Closely associated with this as a great source of hope and comfort is the concept of the coming revelation and glory of Christ that will be revealed or brought to believers with its accompanying deliverance or ultimate salvation (see 1:5, 7, 12, 13; 4:13; 5:1, 10-11).

The 40 Martyrs of Sebastia of Pontus

Let me tell you the story of the 40 martyrs. "These holy Martyrs, who came from various lands, were all soldiers under the same general. Taken into custody for their faith in Christ, and at first interrogated by cruel means, they were then stripped of their clothing and cast onto the frozen lake which is at Sebastia of Pontus, at a time when the harsh and freezing weather was at its worst. They endured the whole night naked in such circumstances, encouraging one another to be patient until the end. He that guarded them, named Aglaius, who was commanded to receive any of them that might deny Christ, had a vision in which he saw heavenly powers distributing crowns to all of the Martyrs, except one, who soon after abandoned the contest. Seeing this, Aglaius professed himself a Christian and joined the Martyrs on the lake, and the number of forty remained complete. In the morning, when they were almost dead from the cold, they were cast into fire, after which their remains were thrown into the river. Thus they finished the good course of martyrdom in 320 A.D.

Peter denying Jesus to a servant girl

How is it that Peter, a follower of Christ can go from staying by the fire to warm himself and denying Jesus with curses before a servant girl to becoming men and women who would defy all that their government would throw at them? They had the example of Jesus who would die following the sham of a legal trial because he was righteous. Righteousness is an affront to an unrighteous world. 350 years before Jesus, the Greek philosopher Socrates observed, "The just man, then, as we have pictured him, will be scourged, tortured, and imprisoned, his eyes will be put out, and after enduring every humiliation he will be crucified, and learn at last that in the world as it is we should want not to be, but to seem, just." But it was more that the inconvenience of a righteous man, it was a righteous man who died for the unrighteous, that he would make them friends of God. It didn't matter whether it was a Jewish fisherman, or gentile slave girls or a hardened legionnaire. Grace and peace in abundance was offered to all men and women, high and low as it is still presented and represented to this day.

## Point 3. Saved by Baptism

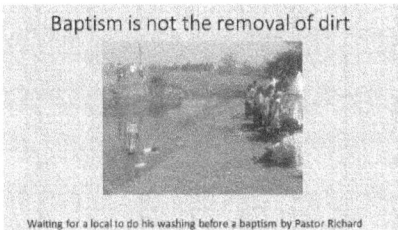

Baptism is not the removal of dirt

Waiting for a local to do his washing before a baptism by Pastor Richard

But it is more than a righteous man dying for the unrighteous. It was a righteous man condemned under the so-called righteousness this world offers but made alive by the Spirit. But it is even more than that. This very same Spirit that quickened the lifeless body of Jesus came to live in all these saints, from high to low. And Peter said to his hearers, in verse 22 that it is baptism that saves you. The young slave girls and the forty legionnaires might say, in a sense, that that it was baptism that condemned them. It was this sacrament, not an oath to do good works, that proclaimed before friend and foe alike that they were disciples of Christ. Peter looked at the example of Noah's flood and saw in the deluge both salvation and condemnation for an understanding of baptism. The waters bought salvation for those eight who heard the preaching of Noah and believed and destruction for those who rejected the word he preached.

So, do you have to be baptised to be saved? When I was a young man studying in the Church of Christ college in Brisbane, I had lecturers who firmly believed just that. If someone came forward at an altar call, they would recommend that baptism would follow very soon after, even the next day. "What must we do to be saved?" they would quote with the answer, "Repent and be baptised for the remission of your sins." It is not commonly held in that denomination now. There are other verses that could be quoted as well that strongly support this view. We know our Lutheran friends have a very strong view on baptism as well. When I was writing my Introduction to the Sacraments, I had some good talks with my old friend Eric about just this. He put it something like this: "We believe that you are saved through baptism because that is what scripture says." But he went on to say, "but if you are not baptised, you are saved by grace because that is what the scriptures say.' A quid both ways? And yet, though these views from both these groups seem to have a similar ring to them, they were very different. The one baptised solely through obedience, that it was no more than making a statement before others while the other recognising obedience as important, baptised primarily through necessity, because something happened at the time of baptism.

I am not going to tell you what to believe about baptism. If you want to know what I believe read my book. I am quite happy to have a quid each way because I am also very certain that something is left in the baptistry that is never meant to see the light of day again. That a line is drawn under your life at that point. Baptism is not the removal of dirt from the body but the pledge of a clear conscience towards God. It saves you by the resurrection of Jesus Christ, who has gone into heaven and is at God's right hand with angels, authorities and powers in submission to him.

## Conclusion

When John Flynn, Flynn of the Inland, died in 1951 the ABC went silent for two minutes, something that hasn't happened since. Now the death of a church leader, a bishop or an archbishop is more likely to bring rejoicing. It may well be that righteous life has been an inconvenient truth that shone a light on their own hostility to God and his ways but, increasingly, the derision has been deserved. Irrelevance rather than persecution is most likely to be the lot of Christianity in this country for the foreseeable future. Never has it been more important to live the life of Christ in the power of his Spirit.

Remember the source of this life. The saints that lived in Pontus, Galatia, Cappadocia, Asia and Bithynia were not the elite that had pulled themselves up by their own bootstraps and adopted a better philosophy from among the many that competed for the hearts of men. They had chosen a life of grace and peace in abundance because they had listened and responded to the word preached about a righteous man, a man whom they worshiped as God, a man who lived a life so righteous that an ungodly world did all it could to extinguish it.

This man gave them a new life in this world, a new start whereby their sins were forgiven and the same Spirit that made this righteous man alive came to live in them as well. There had to be something different about the life they now lived. It is a life for servant girls and legionaries and farmers and accountants. It is a life for housewives and teachers and even sawmillers and pastors. It is a life of grace and peace in abundance whatever the future.

# 11 JOSEPH

*This sermon was preached at Gatton Church of Christ in the lead up to Christmas. Their pastor and my friend Barry Benz was away. On paper, it looked like the worst sermon I had prepared for a long time but, for all that, seemed to be a blessing.*

**Reading:** Matthew 1:17-25

¹⁷ Thus there were fourteen generations in all from Abraham to David, fourteen from David to the exile to Babylon and fourteen from the exile to the Messiah.

*Joseph Accepts Jesus as His Son*

¹⁸ This is how the birth of Jesus the Messiah came about[d]: His mother Mary was pledged to be married to Joseph, but before they came together, she was found to be pregnant through the Holy Spirit. ¹⁹ Because Joseph, her husband was faithful to the law, and yet[e] did not want to expose her to public disgrace, he had in mind to divorce her quietly.

²⁰ But after he had considered this, an angel of the Lord appeared to him in a dream and said, "Joseph son of David, do not be afraid to take Mary home as your wife, because what is conceived in her is from the Holy Spirit. ²¹ She will give birth to a son, and you are to give him the name Jesus,[f] because he will save his people from their sins."

²² All this took place to fulfil what the Lord had said through the prophet: ²³ "The virgin will conceive and give birth to a son, and they will call him Immanuel"[g] (which means "God with us").

²⁴ When Joseph woke up, he did what the angel of the Lord had commanded him and took Mary home as his wife. ²⁵ But he did not consummate their marriage until she gave birth to a son. And he

gave him the name Jesus.

**Text:** Isaiah 11: 1-4 and 10

1A shoot will come up from the stump of Jesse;
 from his roots a Branch will bear fruit.
² The Spirit of the LORD will rest on him—
 the Spirit of wisdom and of understanding,
 the Spirit of counsel and of might,
 the Spirit of the knowledge and fear of the LORD—
³ and he will delight in the fear of the LORD.

He will not judge by what he sees with his eyes,
 or decide by what he hears with his ears;
⁴ but with righteousness he will judge the needy,
 with justice he will give decisions for the poor of the earth.

¹⁰ In that day the Root of Jesse will stand as a banner for the peoples; the nations will rally to him, and his resting place will be glorious

**Introduction.**

As part of your Christmas theme, Barry has asked me to bring today's message based on Joseph. He was a good man, but better than that, he was so good a man the Lord could entrust the most precious gift the world has ever received to his safe keeping. I am going to try to draw lessons from his life to encourage and guide us. We will look at three areas:

- When the world ordered Joseph's life
- When Joseph ordered his own life
- When God ordered Joseph's life

I wonder how clearly Isaiah saw into the future as he looked past his own time to the coming saviour and through to the end of the age, perhaps the time in which we are now living. There is a thing that is called *prophetic vision*. It likens what the prophets saw to someone looking at a series of distant mountain ranges. They can see the main outlines, but they can't see the distance between each range, nor can they see the smaller hills and rivers and creeks in between. Isaiah spoke of Root of Jesse [which] will stand as a banner for the peoples; the nations will rally to him. We look back and see Jesus clearly but what did Isaiah think and what did he see?

Well his mind would have gone to the great king David, the son of Jesse. This shepherd king had a heart so after God that the Lord promised David that his kingdom would never pass away (2 Sam 7;16). Isaiah also knew of king Solomon who started well and finished badly and of Rehoboam whose foolishness divided the kingdom. There were kings in Judah that, in God's judgement, did evil and others that did good. For his own part Isaiah would prophesy under four kings of Judah in the last half of the eighth century B.C. including all or part of the reigns of Uzziah (769 -733 B.C.), Jotham (758-743, regent), Ahaz (743-733 B.C., regent; 733-727 B.C.), and Hezekiah (727-698 B.C.). And while the northern kingdom would fall to Assyria in 722 B.C and be carried away. because of their sin, the eternal kingdom over Judah stood because of a promise given to David. What kind of a king and a lineage did he envisage?

**Point 1. When the world ordered Joseph's life**

Dare I say, the time Isaiah imagined of the Root of Jesse was not one where the line of David as king no longer existed.  The wise men likewise came looking for a palace.  It would not have been a time when all the royal money had gone nor a time when all the glory had departed.  When Joseph knocked on the door of the inn in Bethlehem, he could not say, "make room for me because I am of David's direct line.  Here is my gold to pay for the room and to pay for my retinue of servants and guards."  Any claim Joseph may have had to royalty had long gone and he would have to be grateful for space in the stable instead of his wife Mary giving birth in the street.  All memory of him and his family had passed. It appears he could not even call on family in his ancestral home.

But Joseph was faithful despite the promises of God pointing to a life of ease and prosperity and of authority for his family line having long disappeared.  Instead, he found himself at the beck and call of Caesar Augustus and Quirinius, governor of Syria.  While the past glory had gone, God's purposes hadn't failed but remained certain, though hidden.  He was faithful even though it looked as though Gad had not been faithful to hi promises.  In Matthey 1:17 we read, "Thus there were fourteen generations in all from Abraham to David, fourteen from David to the exile to Babylon, and fourteen from the exile to the Messiah."  Matthew sees in the genealogy, through all the good and the bad, through all the success and the failures, through all the fathers begetting sons, that the history of Israel was running to God's plan not that of an emperor or his a long forgotten governor.

Early in Augustus's reign, Halley's Comet passed over Rome.  Augustus claimed it was the spirit of Julius Caesar entering heaven.  If Caesar was a god then, as his heir, Augustus was the son of a god and he made sure that everybody knew it.  Augustus was no god though he claimed to be saviour of the world. nor even a son of god.  He was nothing but a pawn in the hand of my father and yours.

Did Joseph know the prophesy and understand that the Root of Jesse must be born in Jesse's home town? I don't know, but we do know that emperor, governor and King Herod didn't. Yet, for all their arrogance and their pride, they were, as I said, pawns in the hand of the same God who had been ordering the genealogy of Joseph through 42 generations. 700 years before Augustus made his deluded claims, another prophet, Micah had declared "But you, O Bethlehem Ephrathah, who are too little to be among the clans of Judah, from you shall come forth for me one who is to be ruler in Israel, whose coming forth is from of old, from ancient days." We could easily despair at the way our politics is heading, same sex marriage, abortion up to birth, removal of anything from our Christian heritage, but we must not forget who the true saviour of this world is and, who the true son of god is. And we must not forget how, for all their arrogance and their attempts to control the lives of Joseph and Mary, these small men and women ensured the purposes of Almighty God would be achieved. It has been ever since and will continue to be so.

## Point 2. When Joseph ordered his own life

But our lives are not meant to be always and only ordered by those in authority over us. What can Joseph teach us about how we should order our lives? Joseph was a man who was faithful to the law. The expression of his faith was very different to ours but what was not different was that he was careful about how he lived his life. He looked to something outside of himself for direction and approval for those things that he did right and disapproval for things he did wrong. We would have to look for the Root of Jesse, the child people took to be his, for a sinless life. While we who follow that sinless man look additionally to him for an example and to the Law of Christ, Joseph had the law of Moses as well as the prophets and the writings which showed him how he should live before God and before men. It was never a matter of just

94

doing what was right in his own eyes.

The Law can get a bad rap when we look at the scribes and pharisees who believed they had a claim on God for their obedience to the law. They knew it to the letter and they obeyed it to the letter. God had to approve them and them only, and the rest of Israel, who did not know the law as they did, were cursed. For all their obedience there wasn't faith, just pride. But, of Joseph, it said he was faithful to the law, not obedient. The Law of Moses was not kind to young ladies who were in the predicament that Mary appeared to be in (Deut 22;20). Those who were obedient to the law in Jerusalem had no qualms in stoning the woman caught in adultery. Far away from Jerusalem in Galilee so severe an action was not likely, but the shame and stigma remained.

His actions were different from those who were so obedient. He was not totally blind to the realities of life and he knew that this was not a great start to any marriage. He could have said, "I have been wronged." "I have rights." "My reputation has been sullied." But Joseph, the one who looks as if he has been wronged, looked at how he might protect the reputation of Mary, not his own. "By choosing to divorce Mary privately, Joseph was both risking his reputation as a righteous man within the Jewish community and also forfeiting the financial benefit he would gain through a public divorce. Joseph valued compassion above his own personal interest. Joseph was also willing to risk his own honour after he took Mary as his wife. According to Jewish law, the bride would produce a bloody sheet upon consummation of the marriage as proof of her virginity at marriage (Deut 22:15; P. Ketuvot 1:1, 7-8)."

In one play there are the words, "He is so full of doing what is right that he can't see what is good." The pharisees were consumed with what is right, but that very same law provoked a different response in Joseph. He looked for what is good, something of more value than his good name. We have heard the words of another play, this time from Shakespeare:

Who steals my purse steals trash; 'tis something, nothing;
'Twas mine, 'tis his, and has been slave to thousands;
But he that filches from me my good name
Robs me of that which not enriches him,
And makes me poor indeed. (Othello Act 3, Scene 3)

But for Joseph, there was a conflict between doing good and having a good name. Joseph had chosen to live a life approved by God, not one approved by men. When it says of the Root of Jesse, "He will not judge by what he sees with his eyes, or decide by what he hears with his ears; but with righteousness he will judge the needy, with justice he will give decisions for the poor of the earth". Surely this was the example he was set by Joseph. Thirty years later when Jesus preached in Nazareth the people of the town wanted to kill Jesus, just like some would have secretly or even not so secretly, wanted to kill Mary. These were not the people whose opinion should have governed Joseph's actions.

This world has become so obsessed with being seen to be good through political correctness and every hashtag it can conceive of, but it does not want to be just but to be seen as just. More than ever in our lifetime, there is pressure to conform to opinions that are contrary to everything that God has said is good and right. We, like Joseph, must be very careful whose opinion we value.

**Point 3. When God orders our life**

Sometimes our actions are driven by the circumstances of life. For Joseph it was a census that he had to comply with. But for most of his life his actions would have been governed by an inner compass.

That compass was informed by and attuned to God's law and for Joseph it was very finely tuned. But that is not the beginning and end of how he lived his life. He also allowed himself and his family to be led by God.

Now, I don't imagine that too many of us have had dream or visons of angels standing beside us and telling us what to do. That is not the point. The point is that there should be an understanding that our life is being guided. And yes, it can be something that breaks into our life completely unexpectedly as it did for Joseph. Some time ago, I was driving at night near Laidley and, as I approached one of the corners a very clear impression came over me, "slow down," which I did, and just then a car came around the corner so fast that it drifted into my land and took out my driver's side mirror. But that is not how I am normally led, or how you are led on a daily basis. But make no mistake. Our Lord has promised not to leave us to own devices but to lead us. Verses like, "Trust in the LORD with all your heart and do not lean on your own understanding. In all your ways acknowledge Him, and He will make your paths straight." (Proverbs 3:5-6) would have been known to Joseph. The root of Jesse, like the great king David would call himself a shepherd, yes, he nurtures his own but he also protects and leads.

As a young man or woman standing and staring into the future, how do you make decisions? You can't see what is ahead of you tomorrow, let alone 40 or 50 years ahead. But there is one who can. There is one who can be trusted to lead you. It won't be as he led Joseph, nor will it be as he led me, but the shepherd of your soul will lead you. We who are older and looking back can with certainty say he has directed our path.

Just as the Almighty did not leave Joseph to flounder in those dark days, he has promised to lead us, through good and ill. Some years ago, I stood at the grave of King George VI and Queen Elizabeth, the Queen Mother and read their epitaph which was a poem he read to the empire in his Christmas address in 1939 at the beginning of World War Two.

And I said to the man who stood at the gate of the year:
"Give me a light that I may tread safely into the unknown."
And he replied:
"Go out into the darkness and put your hand into the Hand of God.
That shall be to you better than light and safer than a known way."
So I went forth, and finding the Hand of God, trod gladly into the night.
And He led me towards the hills and the breaking of day in the lone East.

I am convinced of this truth as I hope you are.

## Conclusion

Joseph lived his life very carefully and sought to live a life that brought God's approval, not the approval of others. He lived seeking what was the best for others even if it was at his own expense. This is a life we can all live because the Spirit of God lives in us and has promised to lead us into the knowledge of Jesus. We, like Joseph, also have to deal with circumstances around us that can look so out of control and are certainly far from the way we would engineer them, but our Lord and God has promised to work them for good if you love Joseph's son, the Root of Jesse. Finally, we are promised to be cared for and led with love by a shepherd that knows our name.

# 12 MONERGISM

**Reading:** Genesis 15 The Lord's Covenant with Abram

After this, the word of the Lord came to Abram in a vision:

"Do not be afraid, Abram.
  I am your shield,
  your very great reward."

2 But Abram said, "Sovereign Lord, what can you give me since I remain childless and the one who will inherit my estate is Eliezer of Damascus?" 3 And Abram said, "You have given me no children; so a servant in my household will be my heir."

4 Then the word of the Lord came to him: "This man will not be your heir, but a son who is your own flesh and blood will be your heir." 5 He took him outside and said, "Look up at the sky and count the stars—if indeed you can count them." Then he said to him, "So shall your offspring be."

6 Abram believed the Lord, and he credited it to him as righteousness.

7 He also said to him, "I am the Lord, who brought you out of Ur of the Chaldeans to give you this land to take possession of it."

8 But Abram said, "Sovereign Lord, how can I know that I will gain possession of it?"

9 So the Lord said to him, "Bring me a heifer, a goat and a ram, each three years old, along with a dove and a young pigeon."

10 Abram brought all these to him, cut them in two and arranged the halves opposite each other; the birds, however, he did not cut in half. 11 Then birds of prey came down on the carcases, but Abram

drove them away.

12 As the sun was setting, Abram fell into a deep sleep, and a thick and dreadful darkness came over him. 13 Then the Lord said to him, "Know for certain that for four hundred years your descendants will be strangers in a country not their own and that they will be enslaved and mistreated there. 14 But I will punish the nation they serve as slaves, and afterward they will come out with great possessions. 15 You, however, will go to your ancestors in peace and be buried at a good old age. 16 In the fourth generation your descendants will come back here, for the sin of the Amorites has not yet reached its full measure."

17 When the sun had set and darkness had fallen, a smoking firepot with a blazing torch appeared and passed between the pieces. 18 On that day the Lord made a covenant with Abram and said, "To your descendants I give this land, from the Wadi[e] of Egypt to the great river, the Euphrates— 19 the land of the Kenites, Kenizzites, Kadmonites, 20 Hittites, Perizzites, Rephaites, 21 Amorites, Canaanites, Girgashites and Jebusites."

Miss Ryan on a good day

Monergism! Now that's a word you don't hear every day. Monergism, even if we don't know or use that word it shouldn't stump us, at least not if you did derivation under old Ma Ryan. I don't know whether it was the duster flying over my head, the clip under the ear or a tongue that could cut you in two, but something stuck. Let's unstack it: Suffix first, *ism* – action or practice, then the prefix *mono*, one and in the middle *ergo*, I work. There you have it, *the act of one working* or, for our purposes today, *the sole work of God.* Hold that thought because we are coming back to it.

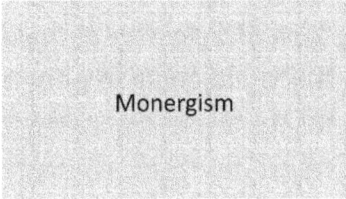

## Monergism

When Pastor Dale asked me to preach on Genesis 15. I thought, finally, something I do not have to think too hard on. I had lectured on the chapter a long time ago and I still had my notes and I also included some relevant parts in my preamble to my book, *The God of Isaac.* How wrong I was, unless, that is, if you want me to replace the clock at the back of the church with a calendar. There is so much here that you could easily spend many weeks in just this chapter. You have the command to Abram (and us) to trust God in uncertain times, you have the problem of unanswered promises and, for Abram, it was of for an heir and the possession of the land. Do you have any unanswered promises you struggle with? We have the most important verse in the whole Old testament for Christians with Abram's imputed righteousness, you have the Abrahamic Covenant, you have respect for human rights, there is the Lord's patience with sinners but eventually judging sinful nations you have God's ordering of this world's history. I could preach on any of these subjects and I would not be amiss, whatever the message it would strike a chord with someone here. For right or wrong, I am still drawn to that uncommon word, but a powerful theme in this chapter, *monergism.*

Don't you start with the best seed?

But first I would ask, why is it Abram, of all the men alive at that time, standing before this bloody scene of the butchered carcases? There were better men, Melchezidec, the king of Salem we are told was better, he received Abram's tithes. If you are going to grow a crop surely you start with the best seed.

The City of Ur

Why did God say to Abram in Ur (Acts 7:20), "Go." Why is it that an old man, from a family of idol worshippers, would leave the 2400 known gods of Mesopotamia to follow the one, by then unknown God into the unknown.

The heavens declare the glory of God

Why? According to Maimonides, a famous rabbi, Abraham vanquished idolatry through the power of his mind, by considering the implications of the heavens and the way they function. To quote the old Rabbi, "He had no teacher, nor anyone to inform him, being deep inside Ur of the Chaldees among foolish idolaters. His father and mother and all the people were idolaters, and he would worship along with them; but his mind searched to gain understanding until he grasped the way of truth, knowing rightness through his correct understanding. He knew that there is one God, and He directs the sphere, and He created all, and in all of existence there is no God but He."

Can the unaided mind of non-believers take them to a belief in God? Surely the answer is "Yes." The theologians even have a name for it, *Natural Revelation.* In Psalm 14, David states that only the fool says in his heart there is no God and, if that didn't sink in, repeats it again in Psalm 53:1. We, like David know that "The heavens declare the glory of God; the skies proclaim the work of his hands" (Psm. 19:1).

The heavens declare the glory of God

Years ago, I had to study the views of the atheist philosopher Anthony Flew on a certain subject. A few years later, to my great surprise, I read in *Christianity Today* an interview with him and how he had rejected atheism and written a book *There is a God: How the World's Most Notorious Atheist Changed His Mind.* Yes, he said, there is a god, the evidence demands it, but, when the reporter for *Christianity Today* asked what this god is like, he basically replied that he had no idea. Reason may, and should, take you to the obvious existence of the creator, but it will never bring you to a saviour. It will never bring you to the one who can call you righteous. In the wonders of the creation God reveals himself, yet he remains hidden. Abram had not discovered God; he had made friends with a saviour and there is eternity of a difference. But why Abram? We are told nothing more than:

Acts 7:2 The God of glory appeared to our father Abraham while he was still in Mesopotamia, before he lived in Harran. 3 'Leave your country and your people,' God said, 'and go to the land I will show you."

This forgotten God of the antediluvian fathers (now that is another word you don't use every day either) singled out one man and appeared to him and, from him, forged a family of faith that would number like the stars of the heaven and the sand by the sea. Abram didn't drag his saviour out of his high heaven by the power of his intellect. it was the sole work of God, here we are back with that word again, monergism, and he said to the most unlikely of men, "Go", and he also said to him, "Walk before me and be blameless" (17:1). There is no one here that has summonsed the creator down from heaven, but the call still comes to a world that has its own multitude of new gods, "Come and walk beside me and be blameless." Many, if not all of you here have heard that call and walked with him for many years. If you hear that voice today understand that this is not your doing. Abram believed God and it was credited to him as righteousness. Some of the old Hebrew texts say something slightly different. Some say, Abram was caused to believe. There is no knowing ultimately which is the right reading, but, make no mistake, that is what happened. The call from knowing a creating God to friendship with a saviour comes from him, respond with all your might.

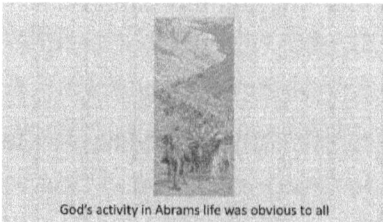

God's activity in Abrams life was obvious to all

Abram had no doubt that the God of this universe had become his friend and had been leading him on a path no man had ever trod before. Long life, great wealth, respect had all come his way even despite himself at times. The creator of the universe called him his friend.

The elephant in the room

To all around him in Canaan it was obvious that this man was different to others but, there was an elephant in the room. The army of Chedorlaomer of Chapter 14 could return, and he may well die a violent death, his flesh be eaten by the birds of the air and his wealth scattered. Even if he would die of old age, he would be childless and unmourned and with no one guaranteed to bury him and still be eaten by the birds of the air. He owned nothing in that land that was promised to him, not even a grave, and an heir would seem an impossibility. Is there an elephant in the room when it comes to your faith? Rachel and I have our son, perhaps it is your health or that of a loved one, or finances. In face of the utter impossibility of it all, the Lord came to Abram and repeated his promise and Abram believed him. The elephant did not go away, and, in Chapter 23, he would have to plead for a grave site in his own land but, despite this, Abram believed God and that was enough to be considered righteous.

Count the stars

His idol worshipping family and neighbours looked to the sun and moon and stars for deities to worship. Others in Sumeria, the home of astrology, looked to their movement to know the future of people and kingdoms. For Abram, he saw neither of these in the heavens but also the father of our faith had no comprehension of what he was looking at. But the God whose hands flung the stars into place knew exactly the vastness of the universe and he said to a childless man your descendants will be like the stars. In Chapter 22, when the promise is repeated it even came with an oath, But the Almighty did not swear by the vastness of heaven which, for all its majesty, is just his footstool, he swore by himself for there was nothing higher to swear by. We could easily have our eyes fixed on the elephant in the room, and I imagine we all have one, but we, like Abram, must get it in perspective. The universe wasn't big enough for God Almighty to swear by to guarantee his promises. For Abraham, the Lord would be guaranteeing his promise offering only himself as surety. We know this same pledge of his own love and honour by his crucified son. Yet his wayward and wilful creation shakes its fist at him and says that even that is not enough, is it enough for you?

Only God can be trusted to keep a promise

More to the point, the question should be, "Can we be trusted?" And the short answer is, "No." Let's return to this dreadful image of the day The Almighty cut a covenant with his friend Abram. And the term is "cut." This whole thing starts with God. I brought you out of Ur, I am giving you the land. Now this covenant comes at God's command, "Take for me a three-year-old heifer, she goat and a ram, also a dove and young pigeon." The first three he cut in the centre and arranged them like a boundary to a path. The whole idea of this gruesome path is that the two parties to the covenant would walk between the severed animals and so acknowledge that, "So be it to me if I should break this sacred promise". But this is not the covenant God made with Abram and so, as the father of our faith, with us. Abram set the scene, and he kept it from violation but at the crucial moment, as the sun was setting, Abram was put in a deep sleep then, what is called a "thick and dreadful darkness, came over him" His family history for the next 400 years is told to him. [17] "When the sun had set and darkness had fallen, a smoking firepot with a blazing torch appeared and passed between the pieces. [18] On that day the Lord made a covenant with Abram and said, "To your descendants I give this land, from the Wadi[e] of Egypt to the great river, the Euphrates— [19] the land of the Kenites, Kenizzites, Kadmonites, [20] Hittites, Perizzites, Rephaites, [21] Amorites, Canaanites, Girgashites and Jebusites."

Only God can be trusted to keep a promise

Of course, Abram meant to walk beside God down the path. But my friends, in the relationship we have with the creator of this universe, there is only one party that can be trusted. He knew out frailty and only bound himself. My friends, don't you see the penalty of a broken covenant in the broken body of Christ upon the cross, and the three hours of darkness that first Good Friday? Not only did the creator of the universe take the obligation for his covenant upon himself, he also took the penalty of its breaches upon himself also. Can we be trusted? The hymn writer said the problem and solution so eloquently:

Prone to wander, Lord, I feel it;
Prone to leave the God I love:
Take my heart, oh, take and seal it
With Thy Spirit from above.

I have said how, in God's revelation of himself in creation, he both reveals and conceals himself. The elements of smoke and fire in this covenant are to be seen again in Sinai in the pillar of fire and smoke. One commentator described it this way, "The heart of fire with a wrapping of darkness shows us the two features of God's divine manifestations. He can never be completely known yet He is never completely hidden." We are blessed to know him, not as the creator but as our saviour and our friend. But how well do we know him? How well can anyone know him?

God is revealed yet hidden

I am reminded of a story about St. Augustine, probably a myth, but the point is valid. For 30 years he had been struggling on his book *On the trinity*, trying to make the concept intelligible. The scene is the seashore, where there is a small pool, a little boy with a seashell, and a sandy beach on which St. Augustine, clad in his religious robes, is walking, pondering with difficulty the mystery of the Most Holy Trinity. "Father, Son, Holy Spirit; three in one!" he muttered, shaking his head. As he approached the little boy, who was running back and forth between the sea and the pool with a seashell of water, Augustine craned his neck and asked him: "Son, what are you doing?" "Can't you see?" said the boy. "I'm emptying the sea into this pool!" "Son, you can't do that!" Augustine countered. "I will sooner empty the sea into this pool than you will manage to get the mystery of the Most Holy Trinity into your head! Upon saying that, the boy, who was an angel according to legend, quickly disappeared, leaving Augustine alone with the mystery of the Most Holy Trinity.

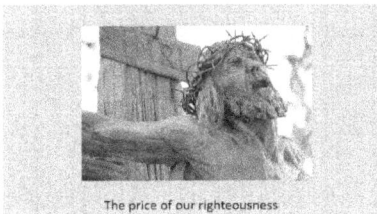
The price of our righteousness

When plumbing the depths of our friendship with the creator we can do no more than empty the sea with a seashell. Should we throw up our hands and say, why bother? We do bother because even the little that we do comprehend is too much for us. We will know more in the next life and I expect be learning of him for eternity. But what we need to know is our friendship and our trust in the creator was not our doing but was the gift of God. He has freely bound himself to us in a pledge greater than his universe. He knows our infirmities and weaknesses and puts our failings to his dear sons account and calls us righteous. My friends, this can only be the sole work of God. Let us then go from this place and walk before him and be holy.

# 13 ECCLESIASTICAL SUPPLY COMPANY

*This is a communion address*

We have lost Tim, our much-loved youth pastor and his family to Mt. Isa where he is taking on his first role as senior Pastor. Years ago, I lost one of my sawyers to the Uniting Church ministry and his first pastorate was Mt. Isa. Rachel and I went up to Mt. Isa to see him. Now, anyone can say we are arriving on the 2.30 flight so I thought I would say something different. On the letterhead of the *Australian Ecclesiastical Supply Company* I wrote a letter something like this:

Dear Reverend Jones,

Regarding your order for ecclesiastical collars, unfortunately you failed to mention the collar height and collar size. As you are aware, the standard height for a Catholic priest is 50 mm and for a Protestant minster it is 38 mm. However, increasingly in the Uniting Church, a collar height of 42 mm is preferred, suggestive as it is of a theological ambivalence.

I will be visiting Mt Isa on the such and such date and arriving on the 2.30 flight. I will bring a selection of clerical collars for your approval.

Yours faithfully,

Etc. etc.

Well, I don't know what his secretary thought when she saw it on the fax machine. Let's be perfectly honest, theological ambivalence is probably not so much the problem now in our community as minds are more and more made up and our heavenly father is firmly seen to be on the wrong side of history. I don't need a saviour. It is all genetic. I don't need a saviour now as I have an illness. How can you say our love is sin? You are the sinner for even thinking it? No, the world is no longer ambivalent. It no longer needs a saviour. We only need saving from an outdated religious superstition about a God who did not exist in the first place.

And yet, every two weeks we come together over a broken piece of bread and a small glass of grape juice and we are reminded, and we accept without any ambivalence, that we are sinners. We don't plead sickness or any other excuse. We take great comfort in our heavenly father who paid the great cost of the death, burial and resurrection of his own son as the only means and the great longing for us to be restored to him. This table is no place for the perfect. God only forgives sinners.

# 14 ISAIAH AND CHRISTIAN MISSION

*This sermon was prepared by Greg Sharpe as an emergency in case Pastor Dale was unable to deliver a Sunday sermon due to ill health etc. This sermon based on a Bible Hour Address at the 2019 Gideon National Conference looks at God's plan for his people, his plan for the nations and the reason why we witness. From his sermon you will see why I call him Gregory of Gatton, lumping him in the same group as the earlier Gregorys of church history.*

Paul exhorted Timothy to "share in suffering for the gospel" and stated that he suffered for the sake of his appointment as a preacher of the gospel (**2 Tim 1:8-12**). What would be the motivation to share in such suffering?

The answer is found in the book of Isaiah which Paul directly quoted 28 times in the New Testament. Paul's first evangelical sermon is found in Acts 13 where he quoted Isaiah **49:6** "… *I will make you as a light for the nations, that my salvation may reach to the end of the earth.*" The leading Jews of the time could not accept fulfillment of this prophecy so it stirred up persecution against Paul. Isaiah was referring to the ministry of the "*Servant of the Lord*", Jesus, but Paul applied the prophecy directly to himself as he was about to extend Jesus' ministry by taking the Gospel to the Gentiles so that God's plan of salvation might reach the ends of the earth.

As Paul wrote to Timothy from a prison in Rome he was passing on the baton and instructing Timothy to pass it on again. The baton was repeatedly passed so that the Gospel would reach the ends of the earth, even Tenthill, but the number of unreached is increasing so we need to accelerate the effort.

This study will take us through Isaiah chapters 40 to 49 where the prophet is preaching to future exiles in Babylon. The preceding chapters, 1 to 39, refer chiefly to events leading up to the captivity in Babylon hence include smouldering scenes of destruction, desolation and exile which are a consequence of future judgement upon Judah. Chapters 40 to 66 contain predictions, warnings and promises which refer to events beyond the captivity and reach on down the centuries through the Christian dispensation.

You might now be wondering about my qualification to be presenting a study based on the book of Isaiah. Unlike most who stand here I have not been to Bible College so I am repeating the content of a study presented by Chris Joliffe at the 2018 Gideon National Convention. Chris is Senior Pastor at Trinity Anglican Church in the Adelaide Hills and was trained at Moore College, Sydney.

There are three aspects to this study:-

1)- God's Plan for His People
2)- God's Plan for the Nations and
3)- Reasons to Witness

Chapter 40 is a turning point from a message of judgement to consolation as God proclaims **His plan for His people**. We begin to read of forgiveness and restoration as in verses **40:3,4** *"A voice cries: 'In the wilderness prepare the way of the LORD; make straight in the desert a highway for our God. Every valley shall be lifted up, and every mountain and hill be made low; the uneven ground shall become level, and the rough places a plain. And the* **glory of the LORD** *shall be revealed, and all flesh shall see it together, for the mouth of the LORD has spoken.' "*

This is a new voice which is not proclaiming a palace for the Lord but a highway in the desert for an Exodus of His people. This is a proclamation of redemption and restoration as God is coming to redeem His people and to bring them home. This is the **glory of the LORD!**

About 200 years after this prophecy, in the year 539 BC, King Cyrus of Persia conquered Babylon. A year or so later he permitted Jewish exiles to return to their homeland. Isaiah's prophecy would have been difficult to accept prior to 538 BC because it would be the first time in history that an exiled people group would be permitted to return to their homeland.

Isaiah previously referred to an exodus in Chapter 35 but he also referred to miraculous healing. **35:5,6** *"Then the eyes of the blind shall be opened, and the ears of the deaf unstopped; then shall the lame man leap like a deer, and the tongue of the mute sing for joy. For waters break forth in the wilderness, and streams in the desert;"*

Again, Isaiah's prophecy would have been difficult to accept because neither the exiles who returned, nor their descendants, saw such miraculous healings UNTIL, about 500 years after the return, there came the voice of John the Baptist in the wilderness; *"He said, 'I am the voice of one crying out in the wilderness, 'Make straight the way of the Lord,' as the prophet Isaiah said.' "* **John 1:23**

With the coming of the Messiah came the healing that was promised about 700 years earlier. The eyes of the blind were opened, the ears of the deaf were unstopped and the lame did leap. God's promises are fulfilled in His time not ours. But not every prophecy of Isaiah had come true with the coming of the Messiah; for example, **45:23** *"By myself I have sworn; from my mouth has gone out in righteousness a word that shall not return: 'To me every knee shall bow, every tongue shall swear allegiance.' "* It is now we who await the fulfilment of promise but about 2,500 instead of 500 years later yet it will be fulfilled because God's Word stands forever; **40:8** *"The grass withers, the flower fades, but the word of our God will stand forever.".* We fall but the Word of God STANDS! This is news for us to share! BUT, do we still believe it when in minority? The Jews in Babylon were a powerless minority in a powerful empire. In a distant homeland God's temple lay in ruins. To the Jews in Babylon, God might have been, merely, an irrelevant idea. We live in a world that challenges the relevance of God and His Word. We can be left doubting the fulfillment of God's promises. This is the reason God poses question after question about whom we really believe Him to be. **40:12-14** begin with the question *"Who has measured the waters in the hollow of his hand"* and conclude with the question *"[who] showed him the way of understanding? "*

By contrast we could ask questions like these:-

- Has the devil measured the waters in the hollow of his hand?
- Has the most persuasive atheist marked off the heavens with a span?
- Has the most innovative mining company enclosed the dust of the earth in a measure?
- Has the most astute political advisor informed God?
- Has the most brilliant scientist enhanced God's understanding?

The questions could go on and the answer is a resounding NO!

From **40:15-17** and learn that even the most powerful of Nations are as nothing before God and regarded by Him as futile and worthless.

The ultimate question is posed in **40:18**, *"To whom then will you liken God, or what likeness compare with him?"*

Would one liken God to an idol that does not fall over?

The point is reached, verse **21,** where God has to ask "Do you not know?" Yes, we do know but we forget so we need to be reminded that *"It is He who sits above the circle of the earth"* and has dominion over it as declared in **40:22-24**.

God asks again, to whom He will compared but this time, **40:26**, declares His dominion over the universe even to the extent that He names the stars.

According to NASA, the estimated number of stars in the Milky Way is between 100 and 400 billion and observable galaxies is 200 billion. God has a name for each star in each galaxy!

According to NASA, if Voyager 1 could continue travelling at its maximum speed of 62,280 Km/hr it would take 1.7 billion years for it to cross the Milky Way.

When comparing God's dominion to ours we could declare in despair: *"My way is hidden from the LORD, and my right is disregarded by my God"* (**40:27**). But we are without excuse! *"Have you not known? ... his understanding is unsearchable."* (**40:28**). God is sovereign over the universe and the microscopic! If it weren't for this fact I would be overwhelmed by the insignificance of my existence.

In times of weariness refresh your soul by returning to Isaiah Chapter 40 and be reminded of who God is.

*"He gives power to the faint, and to him who has no might he increases strength. Even youths shall faint and be weary, and young men shall fall exhausted; but they who wait for the LORD shall renew their strength; they shall mount up with wings like eagles; they shall run and not be weary; they shall walk and not faint."* (**40:29-31**).

God increases our strength because we have a part to play in **His plan for the nations**.

In **41:1** we read of "Coastlands" which refers to the far-off reaches of the Mediterranean (towards the west) and describes any place that was reached by sea travel.

*"Listen to me in silence, O coastlands; let the peoples renew their strength; let them approach, then let them speak; let us together draw near for judgment."*

The far-off nations were those most ignorant of God and were commanded to meet God at the place of judgement. Cyrus the Persian invaded the Greek Islands in 490 BC. Therefore, in effect, became a judge from the east. He was a forerunner of Christ in the sense that, when Christ comes again, He will judge the nations of the world.

God is going to judge those who oppose Him but not before restoration through "the servant".

*"Behold my servant, whom I uphold, my chosen, in whom my soul delights; I have put my Spirit upon him; he will bring forth justice to the nations."* (**42:1** ) and *"He will not grow faint or be discouraged till he has established justice in the earth; and the coastlands wait for his law."* (**42:4**)

As we move to **42:5** we read of God giving breath to all people, that is, Jews and Gentiles and therefore people of every belief. All belong to God and His plan encompasses all including everyone with whom we do not identify.

**42:6 & 7** *"... I will take you [the Servant] by the hand and keep you; I will give you as a covenant for the people [Israel], a light for the nations [Gentiles], to open the eyes that are blind, to bring out the prisoners from the dungeon, from the prison those who sit in darkness."* This is revelation of God's plan for all! His **motive** is declared in **42:8** *"I am the LORD; that is my name; my glory I give to no other, nor my praise to carved idols."*

There is a temple in Myanmar, in the city previously known as

Rangoon, covered with gold and diamonds worth billions of dollars. It exemplifies extreme idolatry that glorifies Buddha, a dead man, instead of the living God. God is jealous of His glory and His plan for the nations will bring idolatry to an end.

Move now to **43:20 & 21**: "*... for I give water in the wilderness, rivers in the desert, to give drink to my chosen people, the people whom I formed for myself that they might declare my praise.*" and **43:25** "*I, I am he who blots out your transgressions for my own sake, and I will not remember your sins.*"

God formed and pardoned us for **His praise and glory**, not ours! God's plan will lead to fulfilment of the 1st, 2nd & 3rd of the ten commandments including His declaration of being a jealous God. Does this make jealousy acceptable? No, not for mere man but yes, for the creator and redeemer! God commands reverence and does so through the prophecies of Isaiah.

Go back to **43:10-11**; " *'You are my witnesses,' declares the LORD, 'and my servant whom I have chosen, that you may know and believe me and understand that I am he. Before me no god was formed, nor shall there be any after me. I, I am the LORD, and besides me there is no saviour'*". Who are His witnesses? Those who know and glorify Him. Jesus, as servant, was a witness and He commissioned the Apostles including Paul as witnesses who then commissioned Timothy and so on. Ultimately, we have been commissioned to be witnesses to those who don't know and revere God.

God has granted us a part to play in His plan for the nations and has prepared the way for us: "*Fear not, for I have redeemed you; I have called you by name, you are mine. When you pass through the waters, I will be with you; and through the rivers, they shall not overwhelm you; when you walk through fire you shall not be burned, and the flame shall not consume you. For I am the LORD your God, the Holy One of Israel, your Saviour."* **43:1-3**

The context is witnessing in a hostile world but fear not for He is with us every step of the way.

In chapters **44-49** we find three reasons to be a witness for God.

The question is asked *"Who fashions a god or casts an idol that is profitable for nothing?"* **44:10** After the example of one who uses half a block of wood for heating the question is asked *"… shall I make the rest of it an abomination? Shall I fall down before a block of wood?"* **44:19**

The **first** reason to be a witness is that, unlike an idol, God was not created.

At the end of the chapter, **44:28**, God declares *"… Cyrus, 'He is my shepherd, and he shall fulfil all my purpose'; saying of Jerusalem, 'She shall be built,' and of the temple, 'Your foundation shall be laid.'"* God named, about 200 years in advance, the pagan king who would conquer Babylon and establish a policy that would allow exiles to return to their homeland and to rebuild ruins. The king would be Cyrus and his great, great grandparents would have only been toddlers when this was pronounced. God is in complete control of world history and can therefore be specific when declaring His plan and purpose. We read in chapter **45** of Cyrus, despite his paganism, being exalted by God to the most powerful ruler in the ancient world. *"For the sake of my servant Jacob, and Israel my chosen, I call you [Cyrus] by your name, I name you, though you do not know me. I am the LORD, and there is no other, besides me there is no God; I equip you, though you do not know me,"* **45:4-5** There is no comparison between those, even the most powerful rulers, who merely play a part in history and the Sovereign God who shapes history for His glory.

This attribute sets apart the true God from false gods. In the Quran, for example, there are no specific announcements about a plan for Allah to save his people. God challenges the followers of false gods: *"Declare and present your case; let them take counsel together! Who told this long ago? Who declared it of old? Was it not I, the LORD? And there is no other god besides me, a righteous God and a Saviour; there is none besides me."* **45:21**

God is passionate that He alone be glorified by the nations. *"Turn to me and be saved, all the ends of the earth! For I am God, and there is no other. ... 'To me every knee shall bow, every tongue shall swear allegiance.' "* **45:22-23** This is confirmed again in **48:11** *" ... My glory I will not give to another."*

The **second** reason to be a witness for God is that He, and only He, sovereignly shapes history and, for His glory!

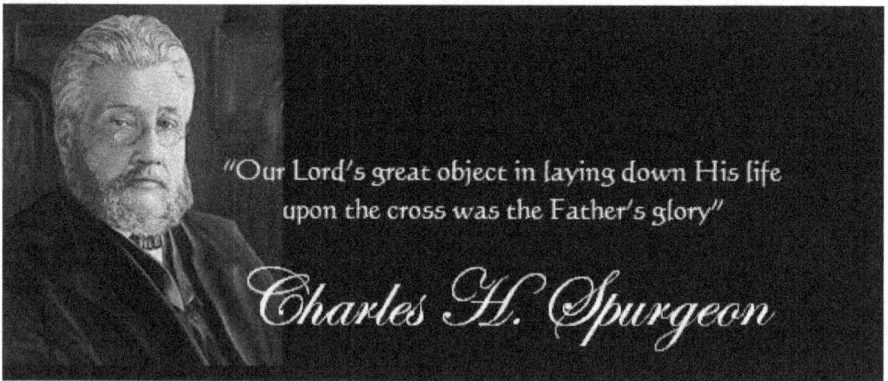

"Our Lord's great object in laying down His life upon the cross was the Father's glory"

Charles H. Spurgeon

We will find the third reason in chapter 49. *"It is too light a thing that you should be my servant to raise up the tribes of Jacob and to bring back the preserved of Israel; I will make you as a light for the nations, that my salvation may reach to the end of the earth."* **49:6** "Then all flesh shall know that I am the LORD your Saviour, and your Redeemer, the Mighty One of Jacob." **49:26b**

God is passionate that He be worshipped as Saviour. That is His plan for His people and for the nations! That is His plan for us as

His witnesses who extend the ministry of the Servant of the Lord to the nations. The motivation is glory to God on the coming day when, at the name of Jesus, every knee will bow and every tongue confess that Jesus Christ is Lord!

The **third** reason to be a witness for God is that only He sends His Servant, as Saviour, to the nations.

Is that what we work and witness for? Is that what we long and live for? That motivation and passion is God's personality hence portrayed in the prophecies of Isaiah. From a prison cell in Rome, Paul shared this passion and through his letter to Timothy we in Tenthill in 2019 hear God speaking directly to us as His witnesses.

I will conclude with **2 Tim. 1:6-8** *"For this reason I remind you to fan into flame the gift of God, which is in you through the laying on of my hands, for God gave us a spirit not of fear but of power and love and self-control. Therefore do not be ashamed of the testimony about our Lord, nor of me his prisoner, but share in suffering for the gospel by the power of God, ... "*

There is no higher calling than to share in the suffering for the gospel for the glory of God!

# 15 RAHAB'S WASHING, IRONING AND MENDING

*This chapter is a ring-in. I delivered it many years ago when I was the Chaplain of the Toowoomba Camp of Gideons International. Unfortunately, one of our members had to be disciplined due to sexual sin. The devotion was addressed not to that brother but to us all. The reading was taken from the daily Bible reading calendar. There has been a long association of Tenthill Baptist Church with Gideons International and presently there are four members and two auxiliary at the church.*

Reading Joshua 2: 1-7.

Then Joshua son of Nun secretly sent two spies from Shittim. "Go, look over the land," he said, "especially Jericho." So they went and entered the house of a prostitute named Rahab and stayed there.

2 The king of Jericho was told, "Look, some of the Israelites have come here tonight to spy out the land." 3 So the king of Jericho sent this message to Rahab: "Bring out the men who came to you and entered your house, because they have come to spy out the whole land."

4 But the woman had taken the two men and hidden them. She said, "Yes, the men came to me, but I did not know where they had come from. 5 At dusk, when it was time to close the city gate, they left. I don't know which way they went. Go after them quickly. You may catch up with them." 6 (But she had taken them up to the roof and hidden them under the stalks of flax she had laid out on the roof.) 7 So the men set out in pursuit of the spies on the road that leads to the fords of the Jordan, and as soon as the pursuers had gone out, the gate was shut.

Have you ever noticed that others are sinners while we just have "weaknesses". The second chapter of Joshua illustrates this point.

Imagine an archaeologist digging up the guidebook for the invasion of Canaan. Plan A is kill all the inhabitants and Plan B is show no mercy. There were to be no exceptions and this was least they entice the Children of Israel after other gods and/or lower the moral standards of God's people. And let's be honest. The picture painted of the Canaanites is not of a pure people. The invasion of the land had been postponed for centuries until their iniquity was full.

So, everything is ready and Joshua sends in the spies and the first thing they do is head for a house of ill repute and stay there for some time. The world's oldest profession in possibly the world's oldest city. Now this should raise a few eyebrows. The ladies of the night heard Jesus gladly but I don't imagine that the spies dropped in to discuss deep truths.

When I was 20 I was driven down Grant's Road in Bombay and saw behind the steel bars of the cages the sad faces of sad women in sad situations. I wonder what Rahab's parents thought of her livelihood? It would break our heart. What did the spies think of her? Very little I expect, as they planned to put her to the sword in a few days.

But disaster looms. The spies are found out and have been observed going to Rahab's house. When all is lost, this outcast from polite society turns the tables and hides the spies at the risk of her own life. Then the meaningful talks did start. She told them that all Jericho knows that that they are facing a supernatural God and destruction is imminent. The residents locked the gates and shook their fist at God but somehow this reject thought, "Maybe God will change his mind and be merciful, the same as the

Gibeonites in Chapter 9.

The spies did give a promise of God's mercy. It was in their interest to do so, and here we are introduced to the "crimson thread". I heard a preacher describe it this way. If we drilled a hole in our bible and inserted a crimson thread through the hole, no matter what page we opened, the thread is visible. Through every page of the law and every harsh command the blood of Jesus cries for mercy.

What about the spies? Moral purity seems to be lacking and understanding of mercy also seems to be lacking except when forced into it. But despite this, they did have integrity as they honoured the crimson thread, What about Rahab? After the promise of mercy there was no sign outside the door saying "Washing, Ironing and Mending Service". There is no indication she did not continue her old ways.

With all her weaknesses, she was declared righteous in both Hebrews (11;31) and James (2;25). God chose this outcast to be the mother of Boaz and so in the line of Christ. To her faith was granted greatness.

Now let us apply this to our brother's situation. Remember the crimson thread passing through every page. We cannot, through the placement of scriptures, offer forgiveness to others if we have not fully forgiven our brother. As for our brother, he needs to hang out the sign "Washing, Ironing and Mending." We should all strive to add greatness to great faith.

# 16 I KNOW A LITTLE GREEK (HE'S A GREAT TILER)

*This sermon was preached by Murray Windolf. He is part of a godly lineage going back to at least Herman Windolf, his great, great grandfather who was the first German Baptist pastor in Queensland – see my book of that name. Murray is a builder and has a sense of humour even stranger than my own.*

Reading: Ephesians 1:15-23

*15 For this reason, ever since I heard about your faith in the Lord Jesus and your love for all God's people, 16 I have not stopped giving thanks for you, remembering you in my prayers. 17 I keep asking that the God of our Lord Jesus Christ, the glorious Father, may give you the Spirit[a] of wisdom and revelation, so that you may know him better. 18 I pray that the eyes of your heart may be enlightened in order that you may know the hope to which he has called you, the riches of his glorious inheritance in his holy people, 19 and his incomparably great power for us who believe. That power is the same as the mighty strength 20 he exerted when he raised Christ from the dead and seated him at his right hand in the heavenly realms, 21 far above all rule and authority, power and dominion, and every name that is invoked, not only in the present age but also in the one to come. 22 And God placed all things under his feet and appointed him to be head over everything for the church, 23 which is his body, the fullness of him who fills everything in every way.*

Now I know you are all thinking 'what is he doing up there?'. Am I right Sam?25 Well I am qualified to speak. I know a little Greek, he's a fantastic tiler and his name is Elias. But on a serious note, how I got to be here was, we go to Gatton Baptist, and a guy was speaking about, pretty much, letting God do what he wants with you. This guy always, sort of, gives the same spiel and each time you can feel God tugging on your heart and I was thinking 'nope

---

25 Sam was visiting the church that day and used to work for Murray some years ago.

I'm not going to give in here'. He said if you feel God's asking you to do something stop saying "No," and I was like, "Aright God whatever it is, even if it's just mowing an old lady's lawn or whatever." The next day, Dale rang me and said, "Would you mind coming out." So, it's amazing how entwined God's family is, even though I was there and Dale was here, and so here I am.

So today we're speaking about prayer, intercessory prayer. Prayer. What is prayer? Is it a combination that you get right, like a safe and then God will open what you are wanting to happen or wishing for? No, prayer is you talking to God and him to you. It is so important to know who you are actually talking too.

One of my last jobs with work was down the coast. It was quite sizeable and hectic. We were living away from home and, true to form, I forgot to pack enough work wear. So here I am, we had to go out and I came back to the job in really nice clothes. There was about 11 tradies on the site and I came in just wearing everyday clothes. There was a Foxtel guy or someone there just running around trying to find a way to bash a hole through a wall and I just came up to him and said you can do this, this or the other. He looked at me and just said 'who are you?'. I just calmly said 'I'm a concerned neighbor, keep going'. Then he watched me talking to everyone and having them all organized and he realized that, hey, this bloke is actually on the ball, he knows what he's doing. So it's the same with us. Sometimes we don't take the time to know God. But he does know what he's doing, he knows every need you have and every need you will have.

We often pray for rain and good health. We pray for the food we eat before we eat, sometimes that's a good idea. But intercessory prayer is when God puts someone on your heart and you pray for their deepest spiritual needs. We all know someone that's either walked away from faith or is struggling. That's the people we need to be interceding for and sometimes even for ourselves. God loves to hear our prayers. He isn't a God that says, 'I'm here, see if you can make it'. This morning I want to encourage you to keep praying for others, interceding for them. And be patient and see what God is going to do because, when God acts, it's right. So often we try and get in there and try and make things happen.

I once went flying through Rosewood.[26] I was running late like always. There was a big sign on the Baptist church that said why worry when you can pray. And I got to thinking that we do both. We spend our time anguishing about something and then we pray but then we keep thinking about it because deep down in our hearts we don't actually feel like God's got it, that he's enough. Life has taught me, when you're praying, thank God for what he's going to do because he is alive and living in us. Don't just pray and think 'Oh well I've done it,' just like (Pete[27] doesn't know this or she probably does), our Tupperware cupboard and when you open it and you need to put more in, you shove it and then shut the door before anything else can fall out. And that's sometimes how we pray, we don't want to be the next one who opens it because it's all coming out. So, you pray, "Dear God do such and such" and then shut the door and then you don't want to hear the answer because, if you do, you might not be ready for it. As I said prayer is a conversation between a believer in his creator. It's a voiced dependence saying, "God I can't. You can."

Again, back to the intercessory prayer. What is it? Do we bother? Or do we look at others and say, "I made it, see if you can" As I was preparing this message in Ephesians 1:15-22 [I realized] it's all about Jesus. It's him giving the revelation, him giving the wisdom. It's he who we are praying to. And it is his life that is living in us. So, we all know someone who needs prayer. Paul set an example of what we should be praying. He wrote a letter to the Ephesians explaining what he prays. I'll just read a few of the verses that I want to talk about. In 17, *I keep asking for the God of our Lord Jesus the glorious father may give the Spirit of Wisdom and Revelation* and then further down *pray that the eyes of your heart might be enlightened.* We need God to reveal Himself to us in wisdom and revelation and [also] for the people who we are concerned about. You notice Paul didn't say, "take away their

---

26 A small town on the back road connecting Gatton, Laidley and Ipswich.

27 Murray's wife

problems." So often when we see people in strife we want to take away the problems and the person will be all right. But God uses those problems. It reminds me of the story of, I think it was, Matty Johns[28] who was touring for Australia in New Zealand. They were touring all the small towns with all their funny names, and they came across one that he said was *tacky wacky*. It was actually *take away*. We so often don't get the point that the problems are there for a reason. We just want to take away everything that's going to hurt us. So when Paul is saying, "God give these people the wisdom and revelation of him", it's like we have glasses and everything we look at in life is through these glasses. We [could] have the spirit of criticism; we could have a spirit of just not caring or apathy but what he's saying is, "Give these people the spirit of wisdom and revelation so everything that comes into life you can see God in it." Things go wrong, God's allowed it. That's okay. He is big enough for it. What Paul is saying in all this is, that God is in this, and I want you to consider all of this in your heart because life is big.

When praying for someone, interceding for someone, pray for the spirit of wisdom and revelation because it is only God that could get through to these people. You might remember Shane Mischke who was here quite some time ago. He said to me once, years ago, "Trotter,[29] you know a lot about God, but you don't know him". That burnt deep into me and set me into a spiral of depression. I was like, God I want to know you for myself, I don't want to know about you. I ended up at Capernwray[30] and then I met Pete, or she met me. It was there when the revelation, the spirit of wisdom and revelation bore fruit of my life where Christ is not just in our head, he's in our hearts to live the Christian life. So, we need to pray for this for others, so that it can change. People that are in need of intercessory prayer, they don't want to be where they are at, they just don't know how to appropriate the life that is in them already. I hope this is making sense. This Bible reading that Dad read out, there is so much in it. It reminds me of the time when Ted and

---

28 A former professional Rugby League player and now media personality.

29 Murray's nickname.

30 Capernwray Australia is a Bible school

Greg and I went to the movies. On the way back home Ted kept saying "there's so much in that movie I want to see it again". It's the same with this reading, there's so much in here. I think it was Gone with the Wind wasn't it Ted? No, it wasn't it was High School Musical 3.

I would like to read verse 17. *I keep asking that the God of our Lord Jesus Christ the glorious father may give you the spirit of wisdom and revelation so you will know him better*. It's all to know God better. When we pray, if you speak what you believe, you're actually compounding your faith. It's the same with the people we're praying for, so that they know God better because when you know someone you trust them. A lot of you are looking at me thinking I don't know you from a bar of soap but, the more you know me, you may trust me or may not. It's the same with praying for family and friends. The reason people do withdraw from God is because they don't know the real God. They don't know him and then they are ashamed or whatever. It's the hope that Paul speaks about later on once our eyes are open to him, that you're comfortable with that hope and they'll grab it. Revelations can only come from God. It's turning head knowledge into heart knowledge. Revelations will affect how you live and what you think, not just what you think.

He goes on to pray that our eyes would be open. In life, problems are allowed in our life so that we actually will see God. In John 9 Jesus actually rubbed mud in someone's eyes so that they could receive sight. Now as an onlooker you would have been thinking what are you doing? Don't you know there's a Specsavers[31] two minutes down the road? In the same way that we watch people in our lives when things are going bad and we jump on the bandwagon and are critical and judgmental and saying what are you doing? God why are you letting this happen to these people? God uses the natural elements of our life. He used his own spit and mud rubbed in this blind man's eyes and he received sight. As for us today, our problems, sometimes they are dirty and dark, but they are what God will use to give our sight because we come to the end

---

31 A national chain of optometrists.

of ourselves and then, there you are.

So, it is important to pray that God will open the eyes of whoever it is you are praying for. Prayer connects God with you and the situation and the person. God is not out there and not interested but he is so willing and wanting to be involved in everything. So, when Dale asked me to speak on prayer and intercessory prayer, I had trouble distinguishing God and prayer because it is the same. God is everything, he is in everything, he is all. I want to encourage you to keep your eyes on Christ and for the people you are praying for that they would see Christ in everything, not to be so caught up in the situations that they are living in but just allow Christ to live through that.

He goes on later in the reading *for the power for those who believe.* Do we believe Jesus is enough for each situation? Do you believe it enough for your family and friends that are in dire straits at times? That is a hard question because sometimes when it's asked of yourself you think 'yeah I do because I'm in control a little bit' but when it's someone else you have zero control. This great power that Paul is talking about is the resurrected life that is given to each believer. By faith it is accessed. We don't imitate Christ; we participate in his life. We're not to imitate, we just get in there and let him live through us.

Unbelief is what kept the Israelites in the wilderness all those years. It's the same for us today. If we are not believing, we do not have the victorious life that he is talking about. Praying for faith in our own life and for others is the doorway for this to happen. God wants us to have an abiding relationship where he is a part of us. Everything we do is Christ in you doing it. Praying, living, working everything. We don't want to be like the Israelites, all those 40 years knowing about God but not knowing him, just like when Shane pinpointed a need in me. There is no use knowing about, it's knowing. As we pray for our family and friends to know God, we're praying that he would open their eyes and give them the spirit of wisdom and revelation so God that can reveal Himself to them, and then they can live the victorious Christian life that

God intended.

So finally, I just want to leave you with the encouragement to keep praying for those who are close to you. Allow God to work, sometimes things don't go the way you expect them to. Keep going. Keep praying. God says keep praying. Pray for the spirit of wisdom and revelation that God would reveal himself to these people and yourself. The more you pray for someone the more you actually believe, "Yes God you are sufficient; you are who you say you are." In your own life, you can look back and think, yes God was there and is every day. God's interested in the smallest things. For example, with work I've been on jobs where, I'm like, "I'm not going to make the deadline". Once we were at Russell Island[32] doing this big concrete job and I took what I thought was enough labour, but the job just kept getting bigger and bigger. Life has taught me to thank God for what he's going to do, because he is interested. I was there tying the reo, Sam knows what that's like, it's not fun. The concrete pump had to catch the ferry across and then everything has to be organized. It has to work like perfectly. I could see it was two o'clock and there was no way we were going to be ready. It's like, "God I don't know what you're going to do, but thank you." Next minute, this old guy walked past, and I thought "What do you want, we're busy". He came up to me and said "Listen, I've been watching you boys all day and you're not going to be ready". I said, 'That's obvious thank you'. He said, "I'm a retired concreter can I help?". I said "Sure, jump on in" and he just came in and took over, got other mates in and we got it done. Then I went back for another job and there he was waiting; he wanted more work.

So, know who you're praying to. God loves us. He's concerned about everything. It is important to pray. We're bringing God into our situation. Don't just plough on through the day thinking I've got this, I can do it, but you can't. Pray for our eyes of our heart to be open and for our family and friends. Pray for belief in him. God is active in our life and alive in our world and our family and friend's world. Don't be discouraged. What you see happening is

---

32 Off the coast of Brisbane in the Moreton Bay.

not the end. God will get through. So on that, I will close in prayer.

Dear Lord, thank you that you are alive and active in our lives. We just give you thanks for what you're doing and going to do. Some of us have a lot of hurt and sorrow that we've watched our family and friends go through. We just pray that you would open their eyes to you, give them a spirit of revelation so that they would see you in everything. I just thank you again for what are going to do in Jesus name. Amen

# 17 THE TABERNACLE OF DAVID

*This sermon was part of a series by Pastor Dale on the Book of Hebrews. While he was away fishing on a "blokes weekend" the passage on the priesthood of Melchizedek was allotted to me. Not the easiest of passages to deal with and I suspect that had something to do with the timing of his trip.*

**Reading:** Hebrews 7: 1-10
This Melchizedek was king of Salem and priest of God Most High. He met Abraham returning from the defeat of the kings and blessed him, [2] and Abraham gave him a tenth of everything. First, the name Melchizedek means "king of righteousness"; then also, "king of Salem" means "king of peace." [3] Without father or mother, without genealogy, without beginning of days or end of life, resembling the Son of God, he remains a priest forever.
[4] Just think how great he was: Even the patriarch Abraham gave him a tenth of the plunder! [5] Now the law requires the descendants of Levi who become priests to collect a tenth from the people—that is, from their fellow Israelites—even though they also are descended from Abraham. [6] This man, however, did not trace his descent from Levi, yet he collected a tenth from Abraham and blessed him who had the promises. [7] And without doubt the lesser is blessed by the greater. [8] In the one case, the tenth is collected by people who die; but in the other case, by him who is declared to be living. [9] One might even say that Levi, who collects the tenth, paid the tenth through Abraham, [10] because when Melchizedek met Abraham, Levi was still in the body of his ancestor.

**Text:** Psalm 110: 1-4
[1]The Lord says to my lord
"Sit at my right hand
    until I make your enemies
    a footstool for your feet."
[2] The Lord will extend your mighty scepter from Zion, saying,
    "Rule in the midst of your enemies!"
[3] Your troops will be willing
    on your day of battle.
Arrayed in holy splendor,   your young men will come to you
    like dew from the morning's womb.[b]

[4] The Lord has sworn
 and will not change his mind:
"You are a priest forever,
 in the order of Melchizedek."

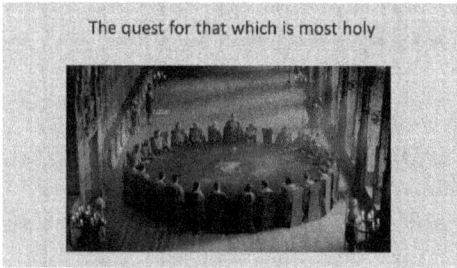
The quest for that which is most holy

**Introduction**

This morning, we are continuing our path through Hebrews which has, as its theme, that Jesus, and his new covenant is better in every way to old covenant. But first, let's do a little imagining. Let's imagine you are a fly on the wall in the court of King Arthur in Camelot. His enemies are subdued and there is now peace in the land, what do you do with a bunch on underemployed knights, You set them a quest of course, to find the Holy Grail, that most holy of Christian artefacts, and return it to the great king.

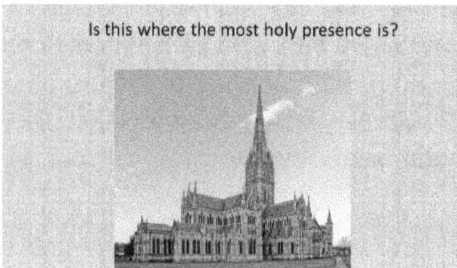
Is this where the most holy presence is?

So, off they set to all corners of the British Isles and Europe to scour the great cathedrals in vain. But one knight remained, Sir Gawain and he has the sense to ask the king just where this holy object might be found.

Or is it just as likely to be found here?

His advice was to cross land and sea and never rest until he comes to the Great Southland of the Holy Spirit and reach the Lockyer Valley. When you get there, hunt through all the farm sheds and make sure you look among the hay at Kilah's, or the parsnips at Winpack or even in Barry and Leone's lettuce.[33]

Well, where is he heading with this? And what has an everyday farm shed got to do with the priesthood of Melchizidek? We are heading there, come on the journey with me.

## Body of sermon

The Arc of the Covenant

Here is something we don't have to imagine, the Arc of the Covenant and the Tabernacle in the wilderness. From Exodus 25 we learn how God told Moses in detail about the design of the tent he was to be worshiped in, and he starts with describing the Arc, the gold covered acacia box with the two golden cherubim on top. The Lord, who the universe cannot contain said to Moses "[22] There, above the cover between the two cherubim that are over the ark of the covenant law, I will meet with you and give you all my commands for the Israelites."

---

33 All church members with farm sheds.

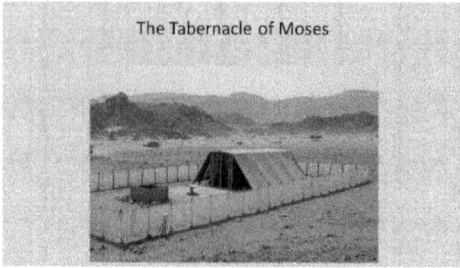

The Tabernacle of Moses

So holy was his presence associated with this box that it was not for the eyes of Israel. It would have to be hidden away, separated by a curtain and only ever accessed by the high priest and even then, only once a year and then only with blood.

The right way to carry the Arc

Yes, the cloud of the pillar of cloud would lift from time to time and the tent would have to be relocated. Then, only a certain group of Levites who had sanctified themselves could carry it. And then only after it had been effectively covered so no one could look on it. So holy was this object that they couldn't even come near it in their travels. Joshua said "When you see the ark of the covenant of the LORD your God with the Levitical priests carrying it, then you shall set out from your place and go after it. However, there shall be between you and it a distance of about 2,000 cubits by measure. Do not come near it." The 40 years in the wilderness eventually passed and the conquest started, and the tabernacle was set up first in Shiloh, and eventually Gibeon.

The wrong way

Now I am going to leave a lot of intervening history out but, one day, King David thought it would be a good idea to load the Arc on an ox cart, despite there being wiser heads that knew better, and bring it to Jerusalem. An early version of Budget Ute Hire. Along the way the oxen stumbled and Uzzah put out his hand to steady the ark and for this irreverent act he was struck dead (2 Sam 6:6-8).

We read in 2 Samuel 6 '⁹ David was afraid of the Lord that day and said, "How can the ark of the Lord ever come to me?" ¹⁰ He was not willing to take the ark of the Lord to be with him in the City of David. Instead, he took it to the house of Obed-Edom the Gittite. ¹¹ The ark of the Lord remained in the house of Obed-Edom the Gittite for three months." If steadying the ark was irreverent, how much more was putting it in a farmhouse.

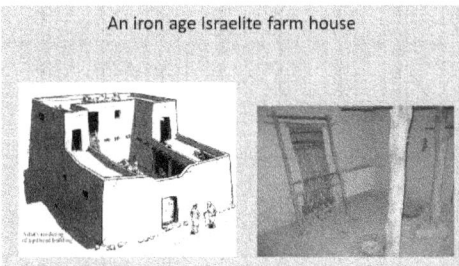

An iron age Israelite farm house

Farmhouses from that time have been excavated and we know what they were like. They combined the barn and animal shelter and often had living accommodation above. There were no fine portal framed sheds and the truss had not yet been invented. Here, we have the most holy object in Israel, and God's who had allowed his presence to be associated with that box, exposed cheek by jowl to the goings in and out of a farm family and their workers and the storage of their crop, I dread to think about the animals also. How different was this to the seclusion and silence of the Holy of Holy's in the tabernacle and how it was explicitly stated that it was to be stored and cared for. It should have been a case of count the bodies but no, the Lord blessed Obed-Edom and his entire household.

Before we move on to David, the Arc in the farmhouse and barn of Obed-Edom urges us to consider where God wants to be found, is it in holy objects? As Baptists I hope we would say, "No." In this building? Yes, but not because of some inherent sanctity associated with the bricks and mortar but because our Lord has promised to be with us when we gather. But what happens when we go out from here to our offices and our fields and our sheds. Have we gone from the holy to the secular? I suspect that if we want to draw that distinction, one that we do see with the Tabernacle of Moses, the Lord will allow us to live that way. But why would we want to when he showed 3000 years ago that he was happy to dwell among the hay and the parsnips and the lettuce and even my books and your office and bless us and our households.

The Tabernacle of David

David heard that the household of Obed-Adom was blessed and he was encouraged to take it to Jerusalem, this way doing it correctly, carried by the Levites. And there he started writing the great psalms that we love today. I was glad when they said to me, "Let us go to the house of the LORD"(122.1), One thing I ask from the LORD, this only do I seek: that I may dwell in the house of the LORD all the days of my life, to gaze on the beauty of the LORD and to seek him in his temple (27:4). How lovely is your dwelling place, LORD Almighty! [2] My soul yearns, even faints, for the courts of the LORD (84:1-2). But there was only problem, there was no temple when David was king, Solomon built the temple. The Tabernacle with its priests was still in GIbeon and the priests were sacrificing there. All the holy furniture was at Gibeon too. All David had was a tent, and the Arc of the covenant. What of furniture? Perhaps there was a chair.

After the prophet Nathan brought him a great prophesy about his throne being established forever we read in 2 Samuel 7 [18] "Then King David went in and sat before the Lord, and he said: "Who am I, Sovereign Lord, and what is my family, that you have brought me this far? [19] And as if this were not enough in your sight, Sovereign Lord, you have also spoken about the future of the house of your servant—and this decree, Sovereign Lord, is for a mere human." There was nowhere to sit in the tabernacle of Moses or the temples, just priests busy about their job of butchery. But in David's tabernacle there were no Levitical priests that we know of, just direct access to the Lord of Glory. He showed himself as someone who was happy for an imperfect king and we presume from the psalms others also to spend time and fellowship with him.

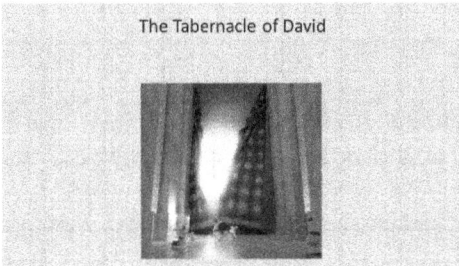

The Tabernacle of David

So, lets recap. So far, we see two paths. One of a formal revealed religion which had the potential to see life compartmentalised into a rigid structure yet with a promise of some sort of relationship mediated by priests. We see also a spirituality found, almost by accident, but a vital one where God is pleased to dwell in the ordinary and, through his presence, make it holy and blessed. It was a spirituality where he is pleased for his children to sit and talk to him without the mediation of a priest. His tent has all gone, a small footnote in history of the people of God. Or is it? Amos, who was active about 760 BC wrote in the ninth chapter [11] "In that day I will restore David's fallen shelter-- I will repair its broken walls and restore its ruins-- and will rebuild it as it used to be." What day was that?  After speaking of God's judgement on the Northern tribes Amos spoke of a time of restoration.

"Behold, the days are coming," declares the LORD,
    "when the plowman shall overtake the reaper
    and the treader of grapes him who sows the seed;
the mountains shall drip sweet wine,
    and all the hills shall flow with it.

Well, such unbounded fruitfulness that follows the re-establishment of David's tabernacle we can't imagine in our drought-stricken land and could easily dismiss it as one of those unfathomable passages from the Old Testament.  Except that is, in Chapter 15 of Acts, James, the Brother of our Lord places it right at the centre of our Christian freedom.  A council was held in Jerusalem to settle the matter of Gentile believers.  And we read [5] Then some of the believers who belonged to the party of the Pharisees stood up and said, "The Gentiles must be circumcised and required to keep the law of Moses."  Peter got up an presented the other side and saying: "Brothers, you know that some time ago God made a choice among you that the Gentiles might hear from my lips the message of the gospel and believe. [8] God, who knows the heart, showed that he accepted them by giving the Holy Spirit to them, just as he did to us. [9] He did not discriminate between us and them, for he purified their hearts by faith. [10] Now then, why do you try to test God by putting on the necks of Gentiles a yoke that neither we nor our ancestors have been able to bear? [11] No! We believe it is through the grace of our Lord Jesus that we are saved, just as they are."  The one side said, "They must submit to the laws, the temple and the priesthood because that is what is written" and the other was arguing, this is what God is doing.

James, mercifully, came down in favour of Peter arguing "[15] The words of the prophets are in agreement with this, as it is written: [16] "'After this I will return
    and rebuild David's fallen tent.

Its ruins I will rebuild,
  and I will restore it,
[17] that the rest of mankind may seek the Lord,
  even all the Gentiles who bear my name,
says the Lord, who does these things'
[18]    things known from long ago"

So again lets recap, God has shown that he is happy to dwell among his faithful and sanctify and bless their daily lives and work, He also showed he could be happy to be approached by his faithful without a priest and without a sacrifice in their hand and for them to spend time in his presence. He declared that this intimacy, though only a brief and obscure part of the Old Testament was to be the model for the church. Do you know this intimacy? A wise man (or woman) would not leave here without seeking it.

## Conclusion

What things did the Lord whisper to the heart of David as he sat in that tent? As David considered that some of his roles were priest like and accepted by God despite not being a Levite, perhaps it was then that his mind was taken back to a Canaanite king from a millennium beforehand. A that once ruled over Salem where he was now king. Perhaps he wondered what it was about this king/priest that Abraham recognised in him his superior yet who in his name *my king is righteous* recognised someone much greater than himself. As a prophet the Lord allowed him to see and speak the things that we heard in our text, things that he could not understand.

The text from Palm 110 takes us back to last week's passage where the writer spoke of the promise to Abraham in Genesis 22 which was guaranteed with a promise and an oath. In Hebrew, the very first word of our Psalm is very, very significant. This is the word of the prophets, "Thus says the Lord", it is a very common word, it is used 360 times and what follows is a promise as certain as God himself. This word is the same one that preceded the oath given to Abraham and here in our text it preceded the promise of the victory of our Lord. What is not common is God himself giving an additional oath. Surely his promise should be enough but, to Abraham, he gave an oath, swearing by himself for there is no one greater to swear by.

In our text also, the promise of a priesthood in the order of Melchizedek is guaranteed with an oath "The Lord has sworn and will not change his mind: "You are a priest forever, in the order of Melchizedek."" The first Melchizedek was an obscure Canaanite king, appearing for only one day in the Biblical record and now lost in the sand of history. But what he represented as a model for the coming king and priest, with a superiority to anything the Abraham or Moses or even his most sanctified Levitical priests could muster. This coming priest we know as our Lord Jesus Christ who went before us into that most holy place, a place far more holy than the mercy seat of the Ark, instead into the heavenly temple of which the earthly tabernacle and later temples were only a pale copy. There he presented his own blood to atone for our sins. The curtain of the earthly temple was torn from the top to the bottom, there was nothing to stop a person from entering, just like the Tabernacle of David.

From last week's passage we read "[19] We have this hope as an anchor for the soul, firm and secure. It enters the inner sanctuary behind the curtain, [20] where our forerunner, Jesus, has entered on our behalf. He has become a high priest forever, in the order of Melchizedek." Our hope is not anchored in this building, or our Baptist denomination, it is anchored in that most holy of places. Where do we go to find it? For those that are trusting Jesus this is no impossible quest because he has come to find us and is pleased to dwell in the ordinary and allow his presence to make it holy. And to that place we are urged to come boldly.

# 18 PRINCIPLES OF LIVING BY FAITH

*This sermon was preached by Chris Meyer and was part of the same series on the Book of Hebrews as the previous sermon  Chris has another sermon in my first book "Sermons from a Potato Field" entitled The Parable of Hank.  Chris is an accomplished rodeo competitor. chaplain and former chairman of the National Rodeo Association .  Team roping his speciality now.  Reference is made in the sermon to his appearance at the 2019 National Rodeo Assn finals where he and his partner won.  Chris is in the white shirt.*

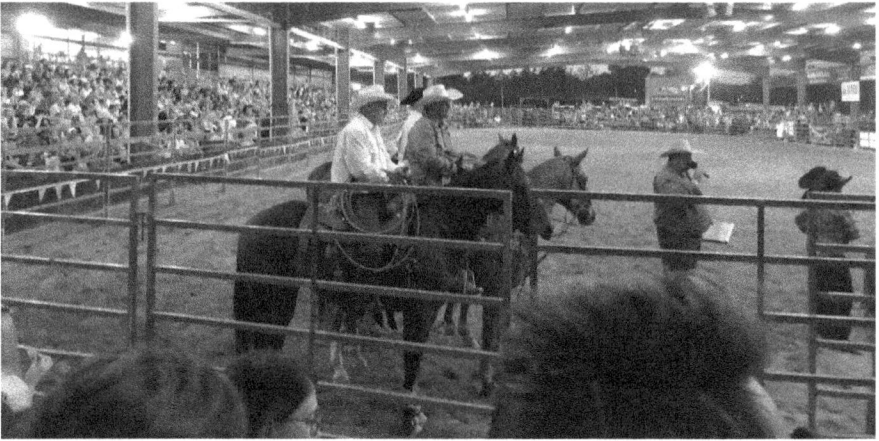

**Reading:** Hebrews Chapter 11.  Now faith is confidence in what we hope for and assurance about what we do not see. 2 This is what the ancients were commended for.

3 By faith we understand that the universe was formed at God's command, so that what is seen was not made out of what was visible.

4 By faith Abel brought God a better offering than Cain did. By faith he was commended as righteous, when God spoke well of his offerings. And by faith Abel still speaks, even though he is dead.

5 By faith Enoch was taken from this life, so that he did not experience death: "He could not be found, because God had taken him away." For before he was taken, he was commended as one

who pleased God. 6 And without faith it is impossible to please God, because anyone who comes to him must believe that he exists and that he rewards those who earnestly seek him.

7 By faith Noah, when warned about things not yet seen, in holy fear built an ark to save his family. By his faith he condemned the world and became heir of the righteousness that is in keeping with faith.

8 By faith Abraham, when called to go to a place he would later receive as his inheritance, obeyed and went, even though he did not know where he was going. 9 By faith he made his home in the promised land like a stranger in a foreign country; he lived in tents, as did Isaac and Jacob, who were heirs with him of the same promise. 10 For he was looking forward to the city with foundations, whose architect and builder is God. 11 And by faith even Sarah, who was past childbearing age, was enabled to bear children because she considered him faithful who had made the promise. 12 And so from this one man, and he as good as dead, came descendants as numerous as the stars in the sky and as countless as the sand on the seashore.

13 All these people were still living by faith when they died. They did not receive the things promised; they only saw them and welcomed them from a distance, admitting that they were foreigners and strangers on earth. 14 People who say such things show that they are looking for a country of their own. 15 If they had been thinking of the country they had left, they would have had opportunity to return. 16 Instead, they were longing for a better country—a heavenly one. Therefore God is not ashamed to be called their God, for he has prepared a city for them.

17 By faith Abraham, when God tested him, offered Isaac as a sacrifice. He who had embraced the promises was about to sacrifice his one and only son, 18 even though God had said to him, "It is through Isaac that your offspring will be reckoned." 19 Abraham reasoned that God could even raise the dead, and so in a manner of speaking he did receive Isaac back from death.

20 By faith Isaac blessed Jacob and Esau in regard to their future.
21 By faith Jacob, when he was dying, blessed each of Joseph's sons, and worshiped as he leaned on the top of his staff.

22 By faith Joseph, when his end was near, spoke about the exodus of the Israelites from Egypt and gave instructions concerning the burial of his bones.

23 By faith Moses' parents hid him for three months after he was born, because they saw he was no ordinary child, and they were not afraid of the king's edict.

24 By faith Moses, when he had grown up, refused to be known as the son of Pharaoh's daughter. 25 He chose to be mistreated along with the people of God rather than to enjoy the fleeting pleasures of sin. 26 He regarded disgrace for the sake of Christ as of greater value than the treasures of Egypt, because he was looking ahead to his reward. 27 By faith he left Egypt, not fearing the king's anger; he persevered because he saw him who is invisible. 28 By faith he kept the Passover and the application of blood, so that the destroyer of the firstborn would not touch the firstborn of Israel.

29 By faith the people passed through the Red Sea as on dry land; but when the Egyptians tried to do so, they were drowned.

30 By faith the walls of Jericho fell, after the army had marched around them for seven days.

31 By faith the prostitute Rahab, because she welcomed the spies, was not killed with those who were disobedient.

32 And what more shall I say? I do not have time to tell about Gideon, Barak, Samson and Jephthah, about David and Samuel and the prophets, 33 who through faith conquered kingdoms, administered justice, and gained what was promised; who shut the mouths of lions, 34 quenched the fury of the flames, and escaped the edge of the sword; whose weakness was turned to strength; and who became powerful in battle and routed foreign armies. 35 Women received back their dead, raised to life again. There

were others who were tortured, refusing to be released so that they might gain an even better resurrection. 36 Some faced jeers and flogging, and even chains and imprisonment. 37 They were put to death by stoning; they were sawed in two; they were killed by the sword. They went about in sheepskins and goatskins, destitute, persecuted and mistreated— 38 the world was not worthy of them. They wandered in deserts and mountains, living in caves and in holes in the ground.

39 These were all commended for their faith, yet none of them received what had been promised, 40 since God had planned something better for us so that only together with us would they be made perfect.

What does it mean to live by faith? In Hebrews 11:6 we find that "without faith it is impossible to please God." Paul goes a step further in Romans 14:23 and declares that everything that does not come from faith is sin." At first glance the writer of Hebrews seems to be supporting a doctrine of faith held by some TV evangelists that faith is a power source of its own. "By faith" Enoch, Abraham, Moses did these incredible things. The thinking is that if we believe hard enough we will see the impossible happen. However if the impossible isn't realized then we are condemned as not having enough faith or there is sin in our life. This is not a Biblical view of faith and it is certainly contrary to what the author of Hebrews wants us to understand about faith.

The heroes of faith weren't commended for their ability to believe but for who they believed in. If I asked you how you came to church today you could legitimately say "by faith". The question then would need to be asked "Faith in what?" And you would say "I came by car." It is not how hard we believe that makes our faith great, it is the greatness of the one we put our faith in that makes the difference.

The first principle I believe the author of Hebrews wants to convey is trusting in who God is. In verse one of Hebrews chapter 11 we read "Faith is being sure of what we hope for and certain of what we do not see." The word "sure" in the Greek is the word *hypostasis*. Bible translators have correctly used words like confidence or assurance however this word goes deeper than just those words at face value. This is the same word the author uses in Chapter 1, verse 3 where he declares that Christ is the exact representation or image of Gods *hypostasis* or being. You see, our confidence or assurance comes out of the essence of the being you put your faith in, in our case Christ.

We can be sure or confident of what we hope for because the one we put our confidence in is trustworthy. He is all sufficient and is able to meet all our needs. It might not be in the way we desire but He is enough because that is His character. He loves us, He died for us and wants to do great things through us.

In verse 3 we are encouraged to believe by faith in a God who spoke words and things came into being out of nothing. All things then are possible when we put our trust in the One who can do the impossible. So how do we increase our faith so we can walk by faith better. The disciples asked that very question in Luke 17:5. Jesus answers "If you have faith as small as a mustard seed you can say to this mulberry tree be uprooted and planted in the sea and it will obey you." To make the impossible happen you only need the teensiest bit of faith. What Jesus is saying to His disciples is that if they are prepared to step out and trust God even with the tiniest bit of faith they will see things happen.

While we only need a tiny bit of faith we do need to build our relationship with Christ in order for us to know Him and know that we can trust Him in our circumstances. Paul tells us in Romans 10:17 that "Faith comes by hearing and hearing by the word of God." The people of Paul's day didn't have Bibles like we do today. The word of God was read to them from a teacher in the synagogue. You could just as easily substitute hearing for reading or meditating or getting to know the word of God so you may get to know Christ better.

However in our walk of faith, trusting in who God is, is only half the story. The second principle the author of Hebrews wants to convey is "obeying what God says". You see, the ability to trust God and to find Him trustworthy is only in the context of obeying what God says. He does this by reminding His Jewish readers of their stories. Stories of men and women of faith who saw God do amazing things through them as they acted in obedience.

I would like us to look at just one story this morning as an example of how the writer of Hebrews brings out these two principles of firstly trusting who God is and secondly, obeying what God says. I have chosen the story of Abraham. His story in Hebrews 11, verse 8 starts with God's call on his life to leave his home and go to a distant land that God would show him and it says he "obeyed and went". In Genesis Chapter 12 we find that the promise Hebrews 11:9 alludes to is that God is going to make a great nation out of this old man and his barren wife. In Chapter 15, verse 4 the word of the Lord comes to Abram again and he reveals that he will have a son from his own body and "Abram believed God and it was credited to him as righteousness".

In Chapter 17, God changes his name from Abram (father) to Abraham (father of many). Now whenever anyone speaks his name they are affirming the promise. Then God makes a covenant with Abraham that every male in his household is to be circumcised that they may be consecrated to God and live under his blessing. He also changes Sarai's name to Sarah and tells her that the promised son will come through her and his name is to be called Isaac which means laughter.

In Chapter 18, we see Abraham grow in his prayer life as he pleads with the Lord over Sodom and Gomorrah. We also see him drop the ball not once but twice, with the King of Egypt and with Abimelech when he told them that Sarah was his sister. The Bible doesn't hide or overlook people's mistakes and that's what makes the book so real and relational, that even Abraham one of the pillars of our faith got it wrong sometimes. I think the point is that the mistakes don't have to define us. It is what we do beyond the mistakes that matters.

In Chapter 21, Isaac is born. God's word came true just like He promised. Joy and laughter comes to this family as they experience God's faithfulness as they trusted in who He is.

We see the pinnacle of Abrahams walk of faith in chapter 22 (Hebrews 11:17). Interestingly it comes in the form of a test. James 2:2 encourages us to count trials as pure joy because the "testing of our faith develops perseverance and perseverance must run its course so that we may be mature and complete, not lacking anything."

God calls Abraham by name and his reply is, "Here I am". While it could signify a servant willing to do whatever his master bids, I think the relationship is to a depth where Abraham knows that he can fully trust God no matter what He asks. And yet God asks the unthinkable, "Take your son, your only son Isaac, whom you love, and go to the region of Moriah. Sacrifice him there as a burnt offering on one of the mountains I will tell you about." What amazes me most about this test is Abraham's reaction. There isn't one. He doesn't chuck a "nana", no complaints, not even a groan or a sigh. The assignment is accepted with whole hearted obedience for he already has God's word that His promise of a great nation is to come through Isaac. In verse 19 of Hebrews 11 the writer wants his audience to have no misconceptions as to the depth of Abraham's faith for he reasons that God would even raise

Isaac from the dead for he knew he could trust in God's word. Abraham affirms this belief (Gen 22:5) when he tells his servants to wait at the bottom while he and his son go up to worship and "we will come back to you".

As they are walking up the mountain things look a little odd to Isaac as he queries the absence of a sacrifice. Abraham response to his son's question is to assure him that God Himself will provide. Here is a gem for us, when God calls us to do the impossible he will also provide the means for that challenge to become a reality. In other words, God is faithful my son, we have only to trust in Him.

When they reach the place, they build the altar and arrange the wood. He then binds his son and places him on the altar. I love Isaac's faith. He could have kicked his old man in the shins and taken off. He chooses to submit, believing in his father and God's promise.

Now the moment of truth. Last night I competed in the last round of the finals in the team roping event. They take the top 12 teams to compete over three rounds. My partner and I were second in the first round and third in the second round. We were leading the average by about four seconds. There is a gold buckle for the header and heeler of the winning team. As I rode into the box for the start of the run, now is the moment of truth. Everything we've worked towards, all the practice, all the miles, the highs and lows all culminate in this one run. Will I stand up under the pressure?

This is the question that is being asked of Abraham. The altar is built, the wood arranged, his son is bound, now the moment of truth. Will he be able to go through with it? Will he trust the Lord enough to obey Him? As he looks at his son one last time, his eyes become blurred with tears. As he wipes them with his sleeve he fumbles for the knife. As his hand clasps the handle he feels its familiar smoothness and the coldness of the hilt. He has used it many times to slay animals for food and sacrifice but now his son. He raises the knife and takes one last breath…

Abraham! Abraham!

Do you notice Abrahams reply? "Here I am". Exactly where I am supposed to be. Trusting fully in who you are Lord, in total obedience to what you have said. I wonder if the Lord was to call your name this morning, would you be able to say, "Here I am." Fully trusting, in total obedience.

And God says to Abraham (Gen22:12) "Do not lay a hand on the boy…Now I know that you fear God." Now I know, what an amazing thing to be known by God. That you were put to the test and you were able to stand.

James 1:12 says "Blessed is the man who perseveres under trial, because when he has stood the test, he will receive the crown of life that God has promised to those who love Him."

In the story of Abraham, as in all the stories mentioned in Hebrews 11, these two principles of faith are evident. Trusting who God is and obeying what God says.

By the way, in the final round of the team roping, we won. To the praise of His glorious grace.

# 19 THE JEWISH QUESTION

*This sermon was preached at the Gatton Baptist Church when most were away at the annual camp. I was given the 'stragglers" to preach to and, as Pastor Doug was preaching through Romans he gave me the next chapter, which dealt with Christians relationship to Jews. Not an easy passage.*

**Text Romans 11 17-32** [17] If some of the branches have been broken off, and you, though a wild olive shoot, have been grafted in among the others and now share in the nourishing sap from the olive root, [18] do not consider yourself to be superior to those other branches. If you do, consider this: You do not support the root, but the root supports you. [19] You will say then, "Branches were broken off so that I could be grafted in." [20] Granted. But they were broken off because of unbelief, and you stand by faith. Do not be arrogant, but tremble. [21] For if God did not spare the natural branches, he will not spare you either.

[22] Consider therefore the kindness and sternness of God: sternness to those who fell, but kindness to you, provided that you continue in his kindness. Otherwise, you also will be cut off. [23] And if they do not persist in unbelief, they will be grafted in, for God is able to graft them in again. [24] After all, if you were cut out of an olive tree that is wild by nature, and contrary to nature were grafted into a cultivated olive tree, how much more readily will these, the natural branches, be grafted into their own olive tree!

[25] I do not want you to be ignorant of this mystery, brothers and sisters, so that you may not be conceited: Israel has experienced a hardening in part until the full number of the Gentiles has come in, [26] and in this way all Israel will be saved. As it is written:
"The deliverer will come from Zion;
   he will turn godlessness away from Jacob.
[27] And this is my covenant with them
   when I take away their sins."
[28] As far as the gospel is concerned, they are enemies for your sake; but as far as election is concerned, they are loved on account

of the patriarchs, [29] for God's gifts and his call are irrevocable. [30] Just as you who were at one time disobedient to God have now received mercy as a result of their disobedience, [31] so they too have now become disobedient in order that they too may now receive mercy as a result of God's mercy to you. [32] For God has bound everyone over to disobedience so that he may have mercy on them all.

## Introduction

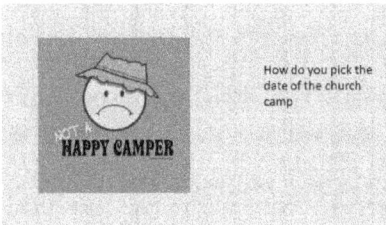

So, it is the annual Gatton Baptist Church camp again. I don't know what process is used to determine the date but I suspect that it is something like this, "I will be up to Romans Chapter 11 on the 27th, that is a great date to go on camp as it is the most difficult part of the book and we can just give that to Ted. Thanks Doug. It is not an easy chapter and I can't do it justice though perhaps we can make just a small dent on it this morning. I have struggled with this message for days, I don't mind telling you, probably because I had trouble making it relevant. In my opinion, theology without application is of little value. With the passing of Dr. Rosenberg, we don't have any prominent Jews in the town (or certainly not many). Whatever Paul says about the subject you could probably even say it has no relevance to us so we can just say the benediction and go home early. We could if it wasn't for the Jewish Question.

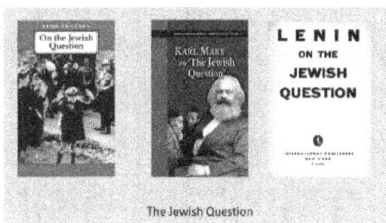

The Jewish Question

"The Jewish Question", the terminology was first used about 1750 in England in debates about the Jew Bill which was passed in 1753. You see, during the Jacobite rising of 1745, the war of Bonnie Prince Charlie, the Jews had proved good citizens and, as a reward, they could apply to parliament for British citizenship. This Act was so unpopular was that it had to be repealed in 1754. The debate around the "Jewish Question" dealt with the civil, legal, national and political status of Jews as a minority within society, particularly in Europe during the 18th, 19th and 20th centuries.

The argument was, so the French proposed, that there was no place in a secular state for those who held religious views and whose ultimate loyalties were to another land. Political emancipation requires the abolition of religion. For Marx, the big issue for a secular state was not religion but the restrictions on freedom caused by economic inequality. And of course, many of the rich were Jews. How things have turned. Our prosperous secular society has led to, in my opinion, political apathy and ignorance. Now Christians, who are citizens of two worlds, are becoming the minority. Now our participation in politics and public life has become offensive and sections of our political elite still look to redistribute the wealth of the nation.

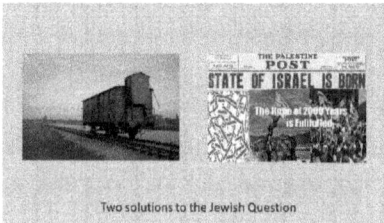

Two solutions to the Jewish Question

Solution after solution was proposed until a new phrase was coined, the "Final solution to the Jewish Problem or the Jewish Question." Depending on who you asked it could mean the gas chambers or it could mean the establishment of a Jewish homeland. But, generally speaking, it was a very dark phrase spoken by men and women with very dark hearts. Too often these men graced a house of worship on Sundays.

## Paul's Jewish Question

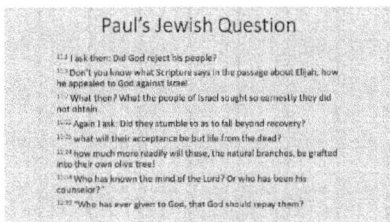

Paul's Jewish Question

But, for the Christian, the "Jewish Question" predates this turbulent time by 1700 years. In Chapter 11 of Romans Paul asks eight "Jewish Questions."

11.1 I ask then: Did God reject his people?

11:2 Don't you know what Scripture says in the passage about Elijah, how he appealed to God against Israel

11:7 What then? What the people of Israel sought so earnestly they did not obtain.

11:11 Again I ask: Did they stumble so as to fall beyond recovery?

11:15 what will their acceptance be but life from the dead?

11:24 how much more readily will these, the natural branches, be grafted into their own olive tree!

11:34 Who has known the mind of the Lord? Or who has been his counselor?"

11:35 "Who has ever given to God, that God should repay them?

| Ethnicity in Romans | |
| --- | --- |
| Ethnic Term | Occurrence |
| circumsion/uncircumcision | 15 times |
| Jew | 11 times |
| Israel | 11 times |
| Israelites | 2 times |
| gentiles/nations | 29 times |
| Greek | 6 times |
| Barbarian | 1 time |
| Total | 75 times |

It would be easy to think that this chapter we are on is something that is tacked on towards the end, or a distraction from the main show that we see in that great eighth chapter. But Paul's letter to the Romans says a lot about race, to the extent that none of his other books use so many ethnic words and particularly the relationship between Jew and Gentiles.

| Ethnic Term | Occurrence |
|---|---|
| Circumsion/uncircumcision | 15 times |
| Jew | 11 times |
| Israel | 11 times |
| Israelites | 2 times |
| Gentiles/nations | 29 times |
| Greek | 6 times |
| Barbarian | 1 time |
| Total | 75 times |

These 75 ethnic terms boil down to two groups, Jews and Gentiles, and more particularly Gentile Christians of which we are a part. And Paul has had a lot to say about these two groups already in Romans. In Chapter 3 both Jews and Gentiles are saved in exactly the same way – by faith and in Chapter 4, Abraham is the father of both the believing Jew and believing Gentile. He takes up the subject of the Jews in Chapters 9 to 11, where we are now and again in Chapters 14 and 15. So what is happening?

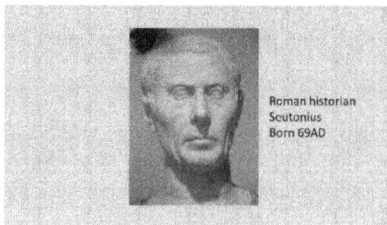

Roman historian
Scutonius
Born 69AD

The church is Rome was not started by an evangelising apostle. We know that there were Jews from Rome who were converted on the day of Pentecost. Best guess is that it was these who started the church in the capital of the empire. The church would have been a Jewish church with some Gentile converts and they would have been considered by the government as a Jewish sect. Suetonius in his 12 Caesars wrote "Since the Jews constantly made disturbances at the instigation of Chrestus, he [the Emperor Claudius] expelled them from Rome. During the reign of Claudius." This was about 49 A.D. Chrestus was a common first name but a pagan would not know the difference between the personal name and Christ. When Claudius died in 54 A.D. the edict lapsed with him and Jews started coming back to Rome only to fine that they were now in the minority in the church. Probably as little as seven years later under Nero's persecution, Christians would be seen as a completely separate group. The church was in the process of finding its own identity. In light of the earlier riots, the returning Jews would most likely want to keep their distance from Christian Jews and for these believers, they had to struggle with the question of whether they were primarily Jewish or whether they were primarily Christian (which would have felt increasingly like a Gentile thing to them). In the light of the church's shameful history, The questions Paul asked deserved an answer.

He begins this chapter by asking, "Has God rejected his people?" This whole Jewish question is much simpler had he said, "Yes." But he answers that emphatically, "By no means." If he has rejected them and his promise to them, he can also reject you who were only joined to him and remain in him by grace, not your own good works and worthy character. Paul speaks about his own position saying I am an Israelite myself, a descendant of Abraham, from the tribe of Benjamin. [2] God did not reject his people, whom he foreknew. He then hits the hearers with the question, "Don't you know the scriptures?" You are not the first to look at unbelief among the Israelites and say they have all deserted the God who called them "his people." A better man than us, Elijah said, I am the only one left. No, no, Elijah, I have seven thousand who I have reserved for myself. You can't see what I see.

So, what about Jews getting converted. Many in the World Council of Churches says it is something we should not attempt to do. Evangelism and conversion are replaced with dialogue and mutual witness which are used to bring the two groups closer together for cooperation on common goals. After all we both want a better world ruled by the same God, we both want justice, peace and the preservation of creation. So, lets chat and get rid of the distorted images we have of each other. Well this is out of keeping with our text, we want a redeemed world. But as a Messianic Jew said, you can't "convert" a believing Jew as Christianity is not a new or a foreign religion. "The first Jewish believers in the Book of Acts did not convert or leave their Jewish heritage to embrace salvation through Yeshua, but simply put their faith in the Messiah."

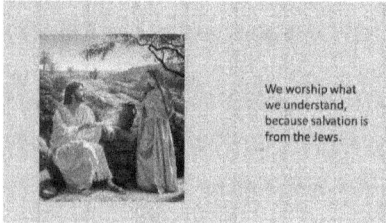

We worship what we understand, because salvation is from the Jews.

Consider the woman at the well in John 4, "[19]The woman said to him, "Sir, I can see that you are a prophet. [20] Our ancestors worshiped on this mountain; but you people say that the place to worship is in Jerusalem." [21] Jesus said to her, "Believe me, woman, the hour is coming when you will worship the Father neither on this mountain nor in Jerusalem. [22] You people worship what you do not understand; we worship what we understand, because salvation is from the Jews."" Jesus stood completely by other believing Jews at the time yet pointed to a coming change in the way God is worshipped, but not the God who is worshipped.

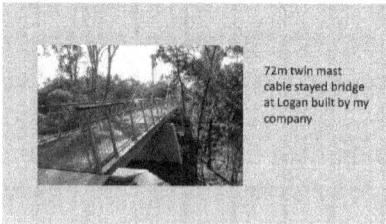

72m twin mast cable stayed bridge at Logan built by my company

Let me try to illustrate this. I used to build bridges and I believe the I built the best steel and timber bridge in the country. Just look at this bridge, isn't it beautiful? But the superstructure is not worth tuppence if the foundations are not right. And these foundations are deep and strong. Christianity is built on the foundation of Judaism and our faith is only a good as its foundation. If we have built on sand, then our faith is without hope, but we stand on the shoulders of giants. Look at the heroes of faith in Hebrews 11 and not one of them confessed faith in Jesus. If we think that there is no access to the father in the Jewish faith post Pentecost, we sadly deceive ourselves. I am presently writing a commentary on the Book of Ruth. I have a number of commentaries that I am referring to but the one I most prize is Jewish. The spiritual insights are very, very deep. Likewise, Paul would boast that he was taught by Gamaliel (Acts 22;3) who was only one of six to carry the title of Raban – our teacher, not rabbi – my teacher and we see his wisdom there.

"What then? What the people of Israel sought so earnestly they did not obtain" but Paul reminded them "The elect among them did, but the others were hardened." In Pisidian Antioch, when the Jew rejected the gospel, we read in Acts 13 [46] Then Paul and Barnabas answered them boldly: "We had to speak the word of God to you first. Since you reject it and do not consider yourselves worthy of eternal life, we now turn to the Gentiles. Salvation always has been God's business softening and hardening hearts as he chooses. "God gave them a spirit of stupor, eyes that could not see and ears that could not hear, to this very day." But we deceive ourselves when we think good works without salvation is just a Jewish problem. Our own secular society which is so proud of its ethical superiority to Christianity is little better to the Jews of Pisidian Antioch. It takes the high moral ground over the slaughter of racehorses but claps and celebrates when it passes legislation approving the slaughter of our most vulnerable. Morality wrapped in either religion or secularism without faith in the living God is an abomination and salvation is only by grace to both.

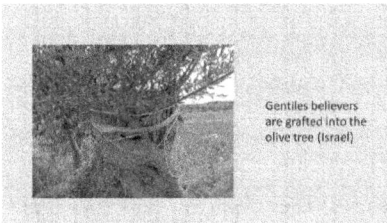

Gentiles believers are grafted into the olive tree (Israel)

Why didn't Israel recognise the hour of its visitation and Paul's only answer is "Who has known the mind of the Lord? Or who has been his counselor?" There is no answer I can give you other than their unbelief. And that is not much of an answer as it God who gives grace to believe. And we deceive ourselves if we believe that we are any better. Paul gives the example of branches from a cultivated olive being cut off and those from a wild olive being grafted in. The olive tree, a symbol of Israel, wasn't uprooted, and unbelieving Christians can be cut of just as readily. But he argues, if a wild olive branch can be grafted in, how much more readily a branch from a cultivated olive. Yes, the rejection of their messiah became a source of great blessing to the gentiles but we as gentiles have not headed Paul's warning

The unbelief among many Jews has led to the blessings of the gospel coming mainly to Gentiles but Paul asks, "Did they stumble so as to fall beyond recovery." Again, No. And the apostle says, "What will their acceptance be but life from the dead?" Jews are not grafted into the Gentile church but believing Gentiles are grafted into Israel, not the land obviously, but into that group of believers stretching back to the Patriarch Abraham. But what we now see in the rejection of their Messiah is not how it ends. Paul asks what will their acceptance be but life from the dead? 25 I do not want you to be ignorant of this mystery, brothers and sisters, so that you may not be conceited: Israel has experienced a hardening in part until the full number of the Gentiles has come in, 26 and in this way all Israel will be saved. And the promise is that when the Jews find their messiah, the gospel blessings will be then poured out in greater measure.

The plundering of the Jewry in Frankfurt, Holy Roman Empire on August 22, 1614

But Lord, forgive me, I do not understand how any Jew would turn to the cross which for millennium has only been a sign of oppression, theft, dispossession, discrimination and murder. Paul warned the Romans not to be conceited when it came to the Jews and this warning was seldom heeded. Standing in the ruins of Auschwitz and other abominations, who could have seen the nation of Israel born in one day yet it as pass, just as the Lord had promised.

The Light Horse memorial in Beersheba, Israel

AUSTRALIAN LIGHT HORSE

While the shameful word Pogrom is etched into the history of Europe and Russia our own national history has been better. Three day before the Balfour declaration on November 2nd 1917 our 4th and 12th Light Horse took the wells of our Patriarch Abraham in Beersheba. Ambassador Dave Sharma at the Battle of Beersheva Commemoration 2015 at the Commonwealth War Graves Cemetery, in Be'er Sheva said "Together, these two developments – the Balfour Declaration, and the Battle of Be'er Sheva – would set off a chain of events that would eventually lead to the creation of the modern state of Israel in 1948."

4th Light House entering Jerusalem 1917

The youngest country in the world liberated Jerusalem two month later. The promise is here in our chapter that the Jews will find their messiah, as unlikely and as undeserved as it is. Unlikely based on our past history. It remains undeserved for the Jews as it is only ever of grace and undeserved on the churches part because of its vile conceit.

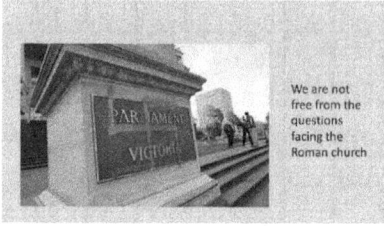

We are not free from the questions facing the Roman church

But we have not been free from anti-Semitism and we have not been free of other forms of racism. I had a good friend who was a Jew and was a child in Belgium prior to World War 2. His father was shot dead in the street by the German. He was one of 12 children and I know what you are thinking, no, they all survived the war, they were farmed out to Christian families who protected them at peril of their own life. We are unlikely to ever face such a challenge to our faith as those 12 families did but we deceive ourselves if we say that dark phrases are not spoken in our land and dark hearts don't walk our street and I have seen it walk the isles of churches. If I can finally give an application to our text, I would point you to verse 14 of our Chapter where Paul speaks of living such a life that it will rouse people to envy so that some will be saved by desiring what you have. Put simply we must we must be radically different to our society and culture.

## Doxologys

Oh, the depth of the riches of the wisdom and[i] knowledge of God!
   How unsearchable his judgments,
   and his paths beyond tracing out!
34 "Who has known the mind of the Lord?
   Or who has been his counselor?"[35 "Who has ever given to God,
   that God should repay them?"[k]
36 For from him and through him and for him are all things.
   To him be the glory forever! Amen.

# 20 A PRAYER FOR THE READER

*The practice in our church is that members of the congregation, not the pastor, lead us in prayer each Sunday. No one brings us into our Lord's presence more closely than Drew Jorgensen who I have asked to write a prayer for you, the reader.*

Heavenly Father we thank you for all you have created.

You took dust from the ground, and like a potter formed it into a man, the pinnacle of your creation.

Your Son, our Lord Jesus Christ, by purposeful miracles, demonstrated your creative power. He healed the sick, gave sight to the blind, made the cripple walk and raised the dead to life.

He loves us and willing laid down his life for us. By his death he satisfied your wrath against sin. He rose from the grave victorious over death.

We acknowledge our rebellion against your holy laws and ask you to forgive us. By faith in Christ we are created anew. Please enable us to be holy and pure like you.

Lord God, thank you for Jesus Christ your Son, the living water, who cleanses us. Now that we believe in Him not only is our thirst quenched, but we receive such an abundant supply of your Spirit that veritable rivers of blessings flow from us.

Lord God, you have made us managers of your creation. May we manage it well and lovingly care for your creatures.

As you cared for the widow, the fatherless and the alien, may we use the gifts you have given us to serve others.

In Jesus name we pray. Amen.

# ABOUT THE AUTHOR

Edgar Stubbersfield (known as Ted) grew up in the small town of Gatton in Queensland, Australia in the 1950's. It was a good time to be young. Life was simple, relatively safe and faith in God was taken for granted. After being thrown out of school in 1965, he started an apprenticeship as a motor mechanic, something he was ill suited to. In 1970, Ted went on an extended trip overseas and was confronted by the Christian gospel in many countries and saw for the first time that there was a God who was alive. That year, he met with Jesus in a Damascus road type experience.

Ministry seemed to be the logical call on his life and he trained initially with the Church of Christ and then in the UK with the Elim Pentecostal Church but found himself most at home with a remarkable group of Grace Baptists. The Lord had mercy on His church and Ted went back to the family business, a sawmill. He kept his interest in Christian faith, living and doctrine by studying by correspondence and by writing. He completed a Master of Theology in Applied Theology in 2011 through the University of Wales.

Ted has a number of other publications but in a very different field - weather exposed timber structures. He is currently working as a consultant in this field.

www.ingramcontent.com/pod-product-compliance
Lightning Source LLC
Chambersburg PA
CBHW021152020426

42331CB00003B/25